D0849314

THE INFORMATION-POOR
IN AMERICA

by

THOMAS CHILDERS

assisted by

JOYCE A. POST

The Scarecrow Press, Inc.
Metuchen, N.J.   1975

Library of Congress Cataloging in Publication Data

Childers, Thomas, 1940-
  The information-poor in America.

  Bibliography: p.
  1. Socially handicapped--United States. 2. Social services--Information services--United States.
3. Social service--Bibliography. I. Post, Joyce A.
II. Title.
HV91.C495   362.5   74-19482
ISBN 0-8108-0775-0

to

THE DISADVANTAGED PEOPLE OF THE WORLD

Thanks to the beleaguered JoEllen Berrettini, Christine DeProperty, Mary Hancock, Nancy Karl, Mary Jane Pietila, Lucy Gilbert Rhoda, Mary Jane Rojahn, Mary Townsend, and Steven Whitman for their steadfast devotion to the bibliographic digging, screening and file-shuffling that this synthesis rests upon. And thanks without end to Joyce A. Post, the one who supervised it all. Finally, my grateful appreciation to the Inter-Library Loan folks at the Drexel University Library.

CONTENTS

I

INTRODUCTION

This is the final report of a study entitled "Knowledge/Information Needs of the Disadvantaged." The work for the study began in June 1972, under a grant from the Bureau of Libraries and Learning Resources, U.S. Office of Education. It was conceived as a review of various literatures. The intention was to produce a digest and bibliography which would help point the way for later research and service. Our method was to survey and consolidate what had been written about the knowledge/information needs of adults suffering from disadvantages of many kinds: age, poverty, handicaps, racial and cultural discrimination, unemployment, and undereducation.

No new data were to be generated. Instead, the job was to uncover and synthesize existing "data." These so-called data could be hard or soft. They could be found in intuitive and expository writings as well as reports of scientific inquiry. The data--and their documents--were not to be limited to any particular disciplines.

We expected the relevant literature to sprawl across many fields of thought, and we expected that literature to be very elusive. We foresaw considerable frustration. Rather than an orderly approach to a well-defined literature by way of indexes and abstracting services, we envisioned something more like an archeological excavation--poking carefully through a great heap of rubble and occasionally coming up

with a relevant fragment. In the end, our expectations were
borne out.

In order to help us bring the "bibliographic dig" within grasp, it was of course necessary to begin defining the
limits of the study. While definitions alone couldn't be expected to eliminate the frustration of scrambling through a
very diffuse and highly fugitive literature, they were necessary for a beginning here, as for any undertaking.

The character of the task is well illustrated in the
title of the study. Three concepts in it cry out for definition:
knowledge/information, needs, disadvantaged--every word except a preposition and an article. The amorphous nature of
the project did more than merely frustrate our progress.
From the beginning it had the effect of reformulating it--
from a straightforward search-and-report to a probe-define-
reprobe-redefine process. Even though relevant documents
were being uncovered from the very first day of the project,
a major activity for the first two months was devoted to setting the limits of the study. In part, this meant defining the
words that title the project; in part, it meant constructing a
model that would guide our search.

A Disadvantaged Person Is ... a Person Who Is Disadvantaged

A person is disadvantaged relatively. His "disadvantage" is a function of a particular context, consisting of his
immediate physical environment, the social norms that impinge upon his daily activities, the economic and political atmosphere, and his internal makeup--both what they are and
what he thinks they are. This is the individual's context.
His "disadvantage" exists within it.

Just as contexts vary from person to person, so also

"disadvantages" vary. A disadvantage for one may not be a disadvantage for another, just because their contexts are separate and different. A society, too, develops its own context--made up of physical and social actualities, social attitudes and values. This is the context that defines "disadvantage" for groups of people.

In contemporary American society "disadvantage" has several definitions, some of which may be contradictory (probably because the society itself is complex and contains a number of contradictory values). One major value in this country at this time--and therefore not surprisingly a major definition of "disadvantage"--is economic. If we had to choose a single demographic variable that would be the most powerful descriptor of those people considered to be "disadvantaged," economic level would be it. Far and away, "poor," "poverty" and "impoverished" are used more than any other single label to define America's disadvantaged.

Yet even defining poverty is a problem. Harrington's Other America clearly illustrates how arguments can rage over the limits of poverty. [1] As much as 25 percent and as little as 13 percent of the American population has been classed as poor. [2] As an expedient, we decided to let the indexes and the literature themselves define "poverty" for us. The target groups or subgroups that were labeled "poor" were accepted as such. Questions arose when a group was not explicitly called poor, but was labeled by another characteristic that seemed to identify it as economically disadvantaged: unskilled, lower class, unemployed, welfare recipient. In general, a document that dealt primarily with people who were obviously at the lower end of America's socio-economic scale was accepted. One that did not, was not.

Racial and ethnic characteristics are regularly part of

the conscious social reality. Consequently, another definition
of "disadvantaged" centers around race or ethnicity. At one
point in our history society deemed the Irish or Jewish Americans disadvantaged for one reason or another. But the patterns changed. Irish enclaves dispersed into the general
population, assimilated "standard" American mores and sometimes achieved high levels of living. Jewish Americans
coalesced. They strengthened their unique culture, at the
same time assimilating the most important "standard" American behaviors and becoming prosperous and highly educated.
In turn, other groups came to be thought of as disadvantaged.
Currently Negroes, North American Indians and several
Spanish-speaking and Spanish-surnamed groups are so labelled
by society.

What does it mean to be disadvantaged? It means to
be lacking in something that the society considers important.
Ordinarily, a city dweller without a horse would not be considered "disadvantaged, " per se. Yet a cowboy without a
horse certainly is. Obviously, a person with no money living
in a culture that values material goods very highly will be
considered disadvantaged. People without health, without
mobility, without specific religious, sexual or other orientations are disadvantaged in a society that values health, mobility, and those specific religious, sexual and other orientations. Women are disadvantaged in a society that esteems
maleness; eggheads are disadvantaged where hardhats are
revered; the aged, where youth is valued.

It seems that everyone is ultimately disadvantaged in
one way or another. If all "who are blocked in any way
from fulfilling their human potential are disadvantaged, " then
it is true; for we each suffer conditions that deprive us of
opportunities, undermine our egos, and limit our physical

capacities.[3]

A conventional definition of "disadvantaged" did not emerge in the course of the investigation. Lists of the disadvantaged, underprivileged or deprived (culturally, educationally, socially, racially, ethnically, economically, etc.) vary considerably. We were forced to manufacture a definition based on our first contacts with the literature. In the end, we decided to focus on those groups that are most often considered disadvantaged by contemporary society, as reflected in the literature. Generally speaking, these are groups that, by virtue of their social, economic, cultural, educational, physical or ethnic condition could be expected to suffer more deprivations than the rest of society:

The poor
The elderly
The imprisoned
The deaf or blind
The undereducated
The unemployed or those employed at a low level (unskilled and migrant workers, for example)
The racially/ethnically oppressed (American Indian, Eskimo, Black, Puerto Rican, Mexican-American).

Of all these disadvantaged groups, the deaf or blind are unique. Unlike the other groups, the deaf or blind person's disadvantage revolves wholly around a physical disability. He does not suffer under similar cultural, educational and economic hardships because of his disability per se. While he may coincidentally share characteristics of disadvantagedness with other groups, his blindness or deafness does not of itself make him comparable. Therefore, except where expressly included, the general discussions in later chapters do not include blindness and deafness as characteristics of America's disadvantaged populations.

In several cases it was known that a "disadvantaged"

group was included in a general population sample; but the report did not analyze for the particular disadvantage--poverty, old age, unemployment, whatever--and the group remained hidden. Since such a document generally contributed nothing to our understanding of knowledge/information and the disadvantaged, it was excluded. Documents that focused on matters related exclusively to the business of being a child or a precollege student were systematically not considered. This had the effect of giving the study an adult cast, but at the same time allowing us to deal with things that apply both to adults and children--such as drug problems or certain kinds of legal questions.

Knowledge/Information?

There are writers who equate learning, education, knowledge and information. There are writers who go to great lengths to distinguish one from the other. As with the word "disadvantage" it quickly becomes apparent that there are no conventional definitions of knowledge or information.

Machlup considers "knowledge" and "information" to be redundant. [4] Shera distinguishes between the two: "The word information is a collective noun for a part of the sum total of that which can be known, and in our opinion it is a misuse to employ it to represent the whole of knowledge. Knowledge, on the other hand, is that which an individual, a group, or a culture 'knows,' and there can be no knowledge without a knower. "[5]

One man claims that information alone strengthens an individual and improves his condition. "Information is power. People will act if they are informed" (620, p. 89). * Another

---

*References in parentheses are to works listed in Chapter VII, Bibliography.

claims that information cannot be separated from the process of transmitting it--that is, the process of educating (405).

Still another claims that information in itself is a "silent" commodity, that "it is the use to which it is put, in terms of inferring, interpreting, projecting, analyzing, manipulating, computing and decision-making, that is important."[6]

For this study, a distinction has been drawn between learning on the one hand and information on the other. Information is seen as the raw material that is used in knowing, making decisions, taking action, thinking and learning. It is the material that is "known"; it is not "understanding." It is discrete pieces of meaningful data; it is not concepts and skills. For our purposes, information is normally limited to that which can be communicated either orally or in written form. The information to which the nose, tongue or fingertips respond has been excluded. So has information in the form of artifacts, visual representation, music, etc.

The provision of information means transferring these discrete pieces rather than acting or providing a concrete service. Providing information includes broadcasting news of a welfare service, publishing a homemaker's directory, telling someone the hospital's emergency phone number. It does not include organizing a community for a welfare protest, authorizing the issuance of food stamps, hiring an applicant, or accepting a child into a day care center.

In sum, the Search has not pursued documents that deal primarily with education, training, learning--formal or informal. Developing the individual's capacity or willingness to remember, infer, calculate, conceive, decide, opine, believe, or do is outside the scope of the project. As well, the literature of services or action programs that does not also consider information per se has not been systematically sought out.

Need: The Recalcitrant Word

Question: Which of the following best defines the word need? (a) Necessity, (b) Obligation, (c) Want, (d) Lack of something wanted, (e) Lack of something required.

Answer: All of the above. Need is applied to a tremendous range of conditions and situations. Society NEEDS better health care. Mankind NEEDS the challenge of unexplored frontiers. We NEED to be better persons. He NEEDS an oxygen tent. The baby NEEDS new shoes. I NEED you!

Need is often talked about. Many documents treat it in many different ways. Quite typical are discussions of felt needs, perceived needs, real needs, postponed needs, etc. In his classic elaboration of needs, Maslow identifies physiological, safety, ego, social, and self-actualization needs.[7] This hierarchy has received widespread attention in several fields where the human element is important--for instance, social services and administration. A variation on Maslow's theme categorizes needs into coping, expressive, contributive, and influential.[8]

Another dimension is added to the discussions with the introduction of "induced felt need."[9] It stresses the importance of acquainting people through interaction with social agencies with certain personal needs that were previously unfelt. Underlying this thought is the more basic idea that needs exist ONLY in interaction with a particular social context, that needs develop only through contact with that context, and that if the context is not the right one, certain potential "needs" will never emerge to the point of being felt.

Fisher emphasizes the importance of need in motivating a person to act in his own behalf. She stresses the idea that the individual must be predisposed to feel a need, and that

objective reality and various predisposing factors and percep-
tions interact to determine an individual's perceived need for
a particular service (216).

Yet few writers deal with the concept of the word itself and what it means. They classify and categorize, elab-
orate and expound, but they rarely explore the nature of the
word. Long provides one notable exception (387). He describes an abstract concept. It is not a concept that flows
from direct observation, the way the concept of apple or the
concept of table does. Need is a construct, an abstraction
that has been developed from a number of indirect observations such as what a person says he needs, or how he acts.

Observing a need is like observing an alpha particle
or the wind. In one way or another they are all invisible.
They are too fast, too tiny, too transparent or too abstract.
So, rather than looking directly at the object--since that is
virtually impossible--we look at the traces they leave behind.

There is at least one risk involved in this process,
though: sometimes it is difficult to determine that what is
being observed is really a trace of the object we are interested in, and not a trace of something else. At times the
trace is clearly linked to the object. (The streaming of a
pennant is "clearly" an effect of a force called wind.) In
other cases we have to make some tenuous assumptions in
order to link the trace to our object. This is particularly
true of the more abstract concepts like need--possibly because their definitions are unsettled. We have to assume
that the traces of need--say, what a person tells us or what
he does--are really expressions of his need and not the expressions of other forces, such as a desire to conform or
to please an interviewer.

All this is by way of saying that need is not a thing

that can be looked directly in the eye. It is a construct and can only be observed indirectly, through its traces. Yet the traces themselves are not necessarily the traces of need, but may be the traces of something else entirely.

Need can be traced in three major ways: what people say, what people do, and what people are. For this study, we have assumed that observing these traces will bring us close to an understanding of need. Specifically, the traces linked to need are:

How people use things--the mass media, informal com-
munication networks, social services, etc.
How people live--habits of economic behavior, home-
making patterns, educational environment, etc.
What people are--conditions of health, domicile, family
and self
What the individual says he needs for himself
What the professional says his client needs
What the expert says society needs.

We must assume that these traces are linked in some way to need. Yet the links are not intuitively obvious. It would be misleading to represent a study of these factors as a study of the abstract concept of need itself. More accurate-ly, our focus is the traces of need among the disadvantaged as related to their universe of information. The emphasis will be on the first four traces: how a person uses things, how he lives, what he is, and what he says he needs.

NOTES

1. Michael Harrington, The Other America: Poverty in the
    United States (Baltimore: Penguin, 1962), Appendix,
    pp. 171-186.

2. Compare Harrington's figures with the U.S. Census Bu-
    reau, as quoted in the New York Times, July 18,
    1972, section 15, p. 1.

3. Mario D. Fantini and Gerald Weinstein, The Disadvantaged:

Challenge to Education (New York: Harper and Row, 1968).

4. Fritz Machlup, The Production and Distribution of Knowledge in the United States (Princeton, N.J.: Princeton University Press, 1962), p. 8.

5. Jesse H. Shera, "An Epistemological Foundation for Library Science," in Edward B. Montgomery, ed., The Foundation of Access to Knowledge (Syracuse, N.Y.: Syracuse University, 1968), p. 12.

6. Oskar Morganstern, quoted in Erich Jantsch, Technological Forecasting in Perspective (Paris: Organization for Economic Co-operation and Development, 1967), p. 95.

7. Abraham H. Maslow, Motivation and Personality (New York: Harper and Row, 1954), pp. 90-106.

8. Howard Y. McClusky, Education Background and Issues, prepared for the 1971 White House Conference on Aging (Washington, D.C.:   White House Conference on Aging, 1971).

9. Arthur Dunham, The New Community Organization (New York: Crowell, 1970).

II

THE LITERATURE

The Search (by Joyce Post)

    Several characteristics of the literature, insofar as they affected search strategy, were apparent from the very beginning. First, the number of documents dealing expressly with the disadvantaged is very, very large. In addition to the ones made obvious by their titles, many more documents contain a section or two on the topic. Even after eliminating the large portion of documents that are rhetoric, what remained were still too many to be examined within the time limits of the project. Second, access to documents through formal indexes is inadequate. And third, many documents with promising titles turned out to be irrelevant when actually examined.

    Indexing in the social sciences has always been less than satisfactory. This becomes even more problematic when new topics or new combinations of old topics appear in the literature. It frequently takes many months, sometimes years, before new topics are recognized in the indexes as identifiable and lasting concepts worthy of their own separate entries. Until that time they are usually put under a more general subject heading and thereby "hidden" to the person searching the index under the new topic only. To retrieve these hidden documents it may be necessary to consult an extensive list of general index terms. This can result in wasting great amounts of time for a relatively low yield.

18

This was one of our challenges. For example, the occasional studies of information needs and information seeking
of people in their everyday pursuits still get grouped, in the
indexes, with the larger body of literature dealing with information needs of men in their professional roles. Or,
worse, they may be hidden under broad index terms such as
"employment" or "housing," with no access whatsoever through
the term "information."

Thus, scanning titles, as was done in Current Contents, was a valuable technique. Another fruitful means of
access, although not too commonly used yet in the social sciences, was through indexes of key words that appear in document titles. Since most access to documents in the social
sciences is still through subject indexes, they had to be relied on heavily. But in a new subject area, particularly, a
title or key word approach will give a higher ultimate yield
even though these approaches may mean many false drops.

With these methods, however, another type of problem
often exists. This is the occurrence of large numbers of
false drops, or documents whose titles seem relevant but
whose content is completely unrelated to our topic. For example, the potentially relevant article entitled "Problems the
Deaf Consumer Meets" was really a description of how a deaf
college student managed to finance her education. [1] It works
the other way too, of course. Relevant documents may be
missed because of the vague general wording of their titles.

Many abstracting services do not lend themselves to
either a subject, title or key word search strategy. Their
entries are arranged by a classification scheme whereby all
documents on the same topic appear together. Since their
indexes are usually inadequate in one way or another, a scan
approach was adopted: relevant sections were located and

the abstracts for all listings within these sections were
scanned.

A fourth characteristic of the literature is that one of
the major search terms, "information," is a word that con-
stantly defies definition. Editorial boards of these indexes
have not been able to come up with a carefully controlled
definition of the term as a subject category. Instead, the
decision to give a document an "information" entry appears
to be based largely on whether the term is used in the title
of the document or on the way the term is used in everyday
speech. For example, providing specific facts on the virtue
of one birth control method over another is spoken of as family planning "information," yet providing specific facts on the
virtue of one food group over another is spoken of as nutrition "education."

An additional problem here is typified by McLuhan's
concept that everything is information.[2] Information needs
are frequently implied in many documents, but the topic, as
such, is very rarely discussed. This means that indexers
and annotaters of bibliographies will not pick up the term "information" and that documents actually dealing with information needs or sources in the area of legal aid, for example,
will be retrievable only through "legal aid" and not "information."

A notable exception to this is Poverty and Health in
the United States: A Bibliography with Abstracts published
in 1967, with two supplements in 1968.[3] In this case, the
abstracters were aware of the information concept and, wher-
ever applicable, mentioned this in their abstracts. This
made this bibliography a valuable source of documents for
further study. A continuation of the Poverty and Health project beyond 1968 would have been most valuable.

A <u>fifth</u> characteristic is that there is little attempt to standardize terminology. Although one of our major focuses was the disadvantaged the word "disadvantaged" rarely occurred. Out of the twenty indexes examined, only five--including two derived from key words in titles--used that word as an index term.[4] Synonymous terms such as "culturally deprived," "culturally disadvantaged," "socially handicapped," "socially disadvantaged," "social deprivation," "economic disadvantagement," "lower class," "underprivileged," "minority groups," and individual terms for each specific minority group are all used in combinations of two or more in each index. Some indexes use both the terms "poor" and "poverty"; others use only one. Some use terms that are too specific: "unemployed" and "hard-core unemployed" are used in one index. Some are woefully behind the times: "administrative remedies" or "administrative procedure" may be used for ombudsman.

All these problems meant that an individualized search strategy and set of search terms had to be developed for each index or abstracting service.

Search Strategy

Getting together the search terms and deciding the strategy to be used for each index was only the beginning.

It was originally decided to search the indexes as far as 1960, but it quickly became apparent that very little had been written in our area before 1968.[5] Primary and secondary search terms were drawn up. Only primary terms were used from 1960-1967; both primary and secondary terms were used from 1968 to the conclusion of the project in the spring of 1973. Primary terms were:

    information
    knowledge
    communication
    disadvantaged, and its various synonyms
    adult

Secondary terms fell into three categories: (1) the various specific terms describing the communications processes and media:

    interpersonal communication
    mass media
    news media
    radio
    television
    television in adult education
    cable television

(2) The various subject areas in which it was presumed that information needs existed:

    consumer affairs
    finance
    family
    homemaking
    housing
    nutrition, family planning, drugs and other health areas
    employment
    education
    social security, Medicare and other welfare programs
    law
    transportation
    recreation

(3) The various specific groups of disadvantaged people:

    urban poor
    rural poor
    blacks
    Appalachians
    migrant workers
    Mexican-Americans
    Puerto Ricans
    Spanish Americans
    American Indians
    Eskimos
    native Alaskans
    Aleuts
    elderly

blind
deaf
prisoners

It should be pointed out that even the above is not a complete listing of all the search terms that were used. Each index had its own synonyms and cross references for many of the above listed terms. Each reference was pursued and examined for all possible relevant documents.

A closer look at this strategy will reveal a Boolean construct with three parameters. Any title with cues that it contained some discussion of <u>each</u> of these three parameters fell within the black area of this figure and was therefore potentially on target. Unfortunately, not many did.

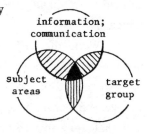

A document that fell within only one of the parameters was automatically rejected. A combination of at least two parameters, as indicated by the lined areas of the above figure, had to be evident before any document was examined. The "information-communication"/"subject-areas" combination was pursued only when it was felt a document might include a discussion of the disadvantaged. Nearly every document located through the "information'communication"/"target-group" combination was examined and accepted. This is an area that until very recently has been almost completely ignored and yet has much to contribute to any serious study of the information needs of disadvantaged adults. The remaining diad, the "target-group"/"subject-areas" combination, yielded most of the documents that were initially located. A good many of these, however, were not explicitly relevant because there was little discussion of an information concept, no matter

how broadly one defines that elusive word. Thus, we were
compelled to make inferences from studies of knowledge,
awareness, and information sources in the various subject
areas.

The Boolean approach was used in a computer search
of the Educational Resources Information Center (ERIC) system. Citations and abstracts for approximately 750 documents
were retrieved, 75 of which were judged worthy of being examined. Of these, about half were accepted for the final bibliography.

While the ERIC system does not include every document ever written, it is a very large national resource of
otherwise fugitive, report-type literature. Its wide scope
and very specific indexing technique, balanced against the
fact that very few relevant documents appeared, strengthened
our original suspicion that few documents explicitly concern
themselves with the information needs of disadvantaged adults.

Poverty and Human Resources Abstracts (PHRA) was
chosen as the first index to check because of the decision to
begin with an examination of the literature of poverty. There
are several unfortunate features of this service. First, the
quality and depth of the coverage and indexing vary drastically
from volume to volume during the seven years of its existence.
Second, PHRA is also misnamed, as it is heavily slanted to-
wards the labor-market/manpower/job-development field.
Third, in the volumes for 1969 and 1970 there were exactly
1200 abstracts and in 1971 and 1972, exactly 1000. This
prompts the suspicion that the size of PHRA is artificially
controlled and as such may not truly reflect the total published literature.

Each indexing and abstracting service was searched
once for all the parameters of the project instead of many

times for each individual substudy--e.g., the health needs of
the elderly, the legal needs of prisoners, or the communication patterns of urban blacks. There were frequently as
many as seventy search terms per index. After all the citations from one index were gathered,
they were first evaluated for their potential relevance. This
was based on which aspects of the project had already been
covered in the literature that had been read up to that point.
In the very beginning everything was read that seemed to de-
vote itself to the topic or subtopic at hand. As time went
on the decision to go to a document occurred less frequently
and qualifications for inclusion in the bibliography became
stricter. After nine months of reading we felt an accurate
report on the state of the literature could be made.

The gathering of citations, the reading of documents,
and the constant evaluation of both citations and documents
were occurring simultaneously throughout all nine months.
Eight graduate assistants were hired to locate documents and
extract relevant portions under guidelines established early
in the project. Constant communication among all persons
working on the project was necessary, of course.

Approximately 3000 citations were gathered. Seven
hundred twenty-five of these were accepted for the final bibliography. Of the remainder, about 45 percent were examined and judged false drops. The other 55 percent were low
priority documents, judging by their titles, and were never
read.

Two other strategies were significant in the search.
The first was semiformal. It led us from the footnotes and
bibliographies of formally retrieved documents backwards in
time to other relevant material. The second, serendipity,
was informal. It allowed us to locate some of our most

relevant documents through such unconventional sources as
"new books received" shelves, runs of bound journals, relevant classification numbers in libraries, news articles in
journals, and just plain nosing around.

Limitations

Time was one of the major limitations. Because of
it the New York Times Information Bank was not searched.
An attempt was made to locate items through the New York
Times printed index, but access was so poor that this source
was quickly abandoned.

Time did not allow use of another somewhat specialized information retrieval system: Project URBANDOC. [6]
This is a demonstration project at The City University of
New York aimed at improving bibliographic services in urban
affairs.   Another information service in this area is Urban
Affairs Abstracts published jointly by the National League of
Cities and the United States Conference of Mayors.   A spot
check of a randomly-chosen issue did not seem to warrant
further searching through the three volumes of back issues.

Two new information services were first issued just
as the search part of the project came to an end.   The first
of these is Update: The Urban News File, published in ten
separate news categories by the Micro Photo Division of Bell
& Howell.   It is similar to Newsbank Index: the user is provided with an index and microfiche copy of articles from 150
United States metropolitan newspapers in each of the ten categories, one of which is "welfare and poverty."   Newsbank
covers only seventy newspapers.   The second new service is
Social Science Citation Index, published by the Institute for
Scientific Information.   All of these sources should be used

for further searching on the information needs of the disadvantaged.

Articles in foreign languages and studies made in foreign countries were not included. There are numerous studies abroad, particularly in underdeveloped countries, of the role information plays in the adoption of innovation.[7] Sociological Abstracts is a very good source for locating citations in this area. (In fact, it was found that nearly all index entries under "information" were to documents of this sort and only rarely to ones germane to this project.)

Psychological Abstracts also has numerous index listings under "information." But here, too, these were nearly all not within our scope. They were concerned with laboratory studies of information seeking under controlled conditions of stress. We were interested in the actual conditions under which the disadvantaged live.

Social workers consider the referring of their clients to the proper helping agency as one of their prime functions. This is spoken of as the provision of information and referral services. A close look at the literature in this area[8] quickly revealed two things: (1) that very little attention is given to the information aspect of such service, and (2) that these services are rarely used directly by the disadvantaged, but rather--if they are intended to benefit the disadvantaged at all--are primarily designed to be used by intermediaries such as social workers or clinic personnel.[9] Therefore this area was not pursued in great depth.

The vast topics of organizing the poor, community development, indigenous leadership and new careers were not actively pursued. However, some documents related to these topics did turn up; they are included in the discussion of "The Political Process" in Chapter IV. Documents that dealt with indigenous neighborhood personnel as information resources for the community were within the scope of the project.

Time and the large number of available documents prevented all-inclusive searches on any one subtopic. Just enough was read to get an overall representation of the topic. We did not search for every document on the need for family planning, homemaking or consumer information by the rural poor, for example. In addition, the final bibliography does not contain every article on relevant operating information programs such as RFD, Operation Gap-Stop or Canción de la Raza. Each document that was accepted dealt in some way --directly or indirectly--with the information needs of the disadvantaged and those that did no more than describe programs were rejected.

And last, we de-emphasized what authorities who work with the disadvantaged write about the information needs of their clients when it is not based on relatively hard data. Categorically excluded were documents dealing with the information needs of social agents serving the disadvantaged. Studies of the disadvantaged themselves and how they perceive their problems and needs were considered more valuable. [10]

The State of the Literature

Every document or document abstract that was judged at least somewhat germane to the information needs of disadvantaged adults was classed according to its overall nature. The primary aim was to discover the relative frequencies of research-based writings, theory and speculation, and newsy, experiential reports. The tally fell out as follows:

Case study	4%
Feasibility study	2
Survey	30
Field experiment	5
Laboratory experiment	2
Digest of research	5
Thought and theory, with some mention of research	20
Thought and theory, with no mention of research	16
Proposal for research	1
Report of a demonstration	11
News article	4
	100%

Since the categories are not mutually exclusive, a certain amount of inconsistency in the coding is inevitable. However, these counts can be taken as an approximate barometer of the literature related to the information needs of disadvantaged adults. Adding "Case study" through "Thought-with-research, " we discover that 68 percent of the documents accepted for the bibliography have a research base of some kind. Approximately 40 percent of the documents--case studies, surveys, and field or laboratory experiments--report newly generated data. About 25 percent--digests and thought-with-research--are efforts to advance theory by dealing with existing data.

As might be expected in an area that is just emerging, the greatest research effort is devoted to describing the real world and establishing the comparatively superficial associations that are permitted by the survey research variables of demography, gross behavior and expressed opinion.

There appears to be a sizeable body of research related to information and the disadvantaged. Yet the whole of it suffers from the same problem that plagued our bibliographic searches: this area of inquiry is not a discrete one. The lack of consistency in the language (for instance, often the

word "information" is not used even when information is the
subject) and the lack of formal access to its literature identify it as an area that--if it were ever to emerge as a fully
adult area of study--is now only in puberty. Its identity is
barely realized by itself, much less acknowledged by the
world at large.

The infantile state of the field is closely tied to a major problem in the researches that have taken place: they
are uncoordinated.   Viewed as a whole, the body of research
is uneven.   It clusters heavily here and leaves gaps there.
It dwells on channel-use or source-of-information studies,
especially consumption of the various mass media; it pays
small tribute to information lack or to the application of information to decision-making.   There has been considerable
study of job-seeking information and very little concern with
local community politics, drugs or alcoholism.

The proportion of demonstration reports and news articles may seem to be surprisingly low.   In this category
might fall reports on community information programs, health
referral centers, televised information programs, hotlines,
crisis intervention agencies, rumor control services, and
many other enterprises concerned--at least peripherally--
with delivering information.   The bulk of the reports do not
deal substantively with information needs.   They merely report on the operations of an enterprise, very often with no
statement of its specific goals and rarely mentioning the needs
of its target group.   (Reports were not accepted for inclusion
in the final bibliography unless they shed some light on information needs.)

NOTES

1.   Betty Hicks, "Problems the Deaf Consumer Meets, "

It is the information that is typically communicated through informal channels outside the disadvantaged communities, or through the printed mass media. It is the information that helps you get to the proper source of help, wield your political power, demand your entitlements--the information that imparts the knowledge needed to secure a share of the standard American dream, to which even the person at the lower end of this society aspires (see 161;420).

The third major barrier to information is a composite of attitudes and philosophies that we will call predisposition. Report after report portrays the various disadvantaged populations as despairing, fatalistic people with a pervasive sense of helplessness. The least disadvantaged individual--suffering from one disadvantage, such as poverty--maintains some hope in the future and is confident that some things, perhaps even things within his power, can be done to alleviate his problem. The most disadvantaged is the one on whom several social and personal disadvantages converge, such as poverty plus poor education plus social isolation plus ethnic discrimination --and who has never known any other way of life. He is the one who is resigned to those conditions of life, convinced that no act of his own will alter them [this discussion draws heavily on a taxonomy of disadvantagedness developed in 274].

Mendelsohn claims that residents of a Denver housing project aspire to what middle-class America aspires to (420). Assume for the moment that these findings are generalizable to most of the country's populations, including all disadvantaged groups: we would expect that the more disadvantaged an individual is--the greater his sense of helplessness, the greater his acceptance of fate--the less effective these standard middle-class aspirations will be in motivating him to act in his own behalf. There is some support for this ex-

Journal of Rehabilitation of the Deaf 6:106-108, October 1972.

2. Marshall McLuhan, Understanding Media: The Extensions of Man (New York: McGraw-Hill, 1964).

3. Poverty and Health in the United States: A Bibliography with Abstracts (New York: Medical and Health Research Association of New York City, 1967-68).

4. The two are Dissertation Abstracts and Sociological Abstracts. The remaining three are the ERIC system, Government Reports Index and Poverty and Human Resources Abstracts.

5. A few relevant documents written before 1960 were uncovered during the search; they are included.

6. Vivian S. Sessions and Lynda W. Sloan, URBANDOC/A Bibliographic Information System, Demonstration Report and Technical Supplements 1 and 2 (New York: The City University of New York, The Graduate Division, 1971).

7. Everett M. Rogers and F. Floyd Shoemaker, Communication of Innovations; A Cross-Cultural Approach, 2d ed. (New York: Free Press, 1971).

8. Eleanor Bolch, Nicholas Long and Jan Dewey, Information and Referral Services: An Annotated Bibliography (Minneapolis: Institute for Interdisciplinary Studies of the American Rehabilitation Foundation, 1972).

9. The findings of one study were typical. In an analysis of callers to an information service only 10.9 percent came from the central area of the city; and less than 10 percent of the known callers were either unemployed, unskilled or disabled. (From Donald F. Bellemy, Information Services; A Study of Information Services for Metropolitan Toronto, a Consultant Report, Toronto: Social Planning Council of Metropolitan Toronto, 1968.

10. This partially explains why the final bibliography contains such a large number of survey documents.

III

INFORMATION AND THE DISADVANTAGED: OVERVIEW

The Culture of Information Poverty

Disadvantaged people share some characteristics that affect their information universe. These characteristics constitute barriers to their felt need for information, their search for it, their acceptance of it, or their use of it.

First, disadvantaged groups are typically disadvantaged by the level of processing skills at their command. Reading ability is very low. Hearing or eyesight may be impaired. English may be a second language. Communication skills, such as those involved in bargaining for a house or budgeting, are not conventional knowledge for them as they are for the mainstream of society.

Second, they are often locked into their own subculture. This removes them from the flow of popular information that exists in society at large. In effect they live in an information ghetto. Their information universe is a closed system, harboring an inordinate amount of unawareness and misinformation (myth, rumor, folk lore). While they do have information contacts with the rest of society, these contacts are very often one-way information flows, via the mass media, from the greater society. It can be expected, where the cultural uniqueness of the group is substantial, that the imported one-way communication runs the risk of being irrelevant or wrongly interpreted. Even more specifically, reliance on television as the primary mass medium--a one-way channel

emphasizing entertainment rather than information--may result in an information void (163;161). While the group may be very rich in certain kinds of internally generated information, it is deficient in the information shared by the larger society.

A study of female public housing tenants in a large northeast city may offer a partial explanation. It was concluded that the poor, even when politically oriented, tend to interact with others largely in a highly personalized or local social milieu. They are not accustomed to dealing with a complex system of specialized role behavior such as a bureaucracy. Thus their interaction with agencies is inhibited, and a potentially important source of information remains relatively unused (372). There is a weaker system of information within the disadvantaged community. Just like most people with a felt need for information, the disadvantaged person turns first to the informal network, the friends, neighbors and relatives who might know. Some of the people who are turned to are "opinion leaders" in the community. Yet while they are indeed more informed than is the person who seeks them out, and do indeed transfer information into the community from outside, even opinion leaders are hindered in fulfilling their role by the social barriers that are drawn up around the community. Although opinion leaders in disadvantaged communities play the same role as gatekeepers in advantaged communities, the former cannot play it as effectively, for their access to outside information is curtailed.

Internally generated information or information specifically aimed at the disadvantaged may accumulate and get disseminated in the disadvantaged community just as it does in every other community. But there is a kind of social embargo against a great body of externally generated information.

pectation in the Warner report. In that study of a sizeable
urban sample, it was found that the poorer and older groups
perceive fewer problems or questions that need to be dealt
with to ameliorate their lives. Those who could be considered personally and socially advantaged express significantly more problems (677). The same study indicates that even
for those problems/questions that they did state, the poorer
and older groups tend to see the problem/question as a need
for information less often than the general population.

It is clear that the disadvantaged are not as predisposed as the general population to alter the undesirable conditions of their lives, or to see information as an instrument
of their salvation.

Information Needs

> "In today's complex society--especially in a
> large urban area like St. Louis with its many
> social service agencies and programs--ignor-
> ance is one of the chief barriers to utilizing
> the resources that are available to meet hu-
> man needs" (5, p. 33).

It is sometimes claimed that the disadvantaged have
information needs just like anyone else. This is only broadly
true. If we look hard enough, we can detect information
needs that are different both in degree and in kind from the
information needs of the general adult population.

Study after study attests to the disadvantaged adult's
widespread lack of information when compared with his "average" counterpart on any number of topics. The studies suggest that all people need essentially the same kind of information to survive in this society, but the disadvantaged individual
needs large remedial doses of information in order to bring
him up to "information par" with the rest of society.

And, as we define "information need" more and more
specifically, a few differences in kind do begin to show up.
Those who are disadvantaged, even though they aspire to the
standard American dream, are impelled by physical, cultural
and personal realities to need slightly different kinds of information. There is some information that he will be inclined
not to need. There is some, and this is the important stuff,
that he will have a greater than average use for.

Considering all people, there are two kinds of information need: kinetic and potential. Kinetic needs are the ones
dictated by a given situation or condition in the life of the individual. They move and change from moment to moment.
If a kinetic need is a felt one, the individual may try to respond to it by seeking out information that will correct a
specific problem, alter a particular reality.

Kinetic needs themselves can be divided into two finer
categories: crisis and non-crisis. Examples of crisis needs
might be "Where can I get some food for my family this
weekend?" or "A rat just bit my hand; what do I do?" or
"My neighbors have left their infant children alone for the
past three days and nights; where do I get help for them?"
Non-crisis needs might be something like "Is there a reading program for adults in my area?" or "Where can I find
a job?" or "What is the address of the welfare department?"
Obviously, crisis and non-crisis needs can be equally important in the life of the needy person; the difference between
the two lies in the immediacy of the need. They are both
kinetic; they are dictated by a given condition or situation.

Potential needs, on the other hand, are only loosely
defined by the present or short range realities. Instead,
they are determined by the longer range anticipations of the
individual. To a large extent, they remain unconscious,

hidden under layers of attitudes, impulses and values that influence the behavior--and specifically the information-related behavior--of the individual. It is a potential need that impels a person to find out who his senator is, just in case; to learn the name of a bail bondsman, just in case; to inform himself on the future of the local job market, or get a physical check-up regularly. Information acquired in response to a potential information need may never be put into action. And, being generally long-range in nature, a potential need can be expected to last somewhat longer than a kinetic need.

Back to the disadvantaged adult. His actions, including his information seeking activities, are directed by his kinetic needs. His unwillingness to delay gratification or plan for even the short-term future militate against his acting on a potential information need. Instead, he will respond to needs that are of crisis or near-crisis nature, for instance, he may seek new housing only after being evicted. He is not disposed to recognize or respond to his own potential (long-term) needs.

More than the average, he feels a need for coping information. Coping with life in the disadvantaged ghetto--urban, rural, black, white, Indian, aged, whatever. This information is the kind that will help him acquire the basic necessities in pursuit of that standard American dream. The information is not frivolous. It is an increment toward action of some sort.

More often than others of course, disadvantaged people have information needs related to public assistance: subsidized housing, welfare benefits, free school lunch, medical care, etc. Closely allied are needs in the area of individual rights--what am I entitled to?, how do I go about getting it?, how do I protect myself legally?, etc. And there are needs

associated with remedial adult education and public day care.
While they are not, strictly speaking, unique to disadvantaged
Americans, these needs to pervade their lives out of all pro-
portion.

Information-Seeking Behavior

There are two kinds of channel by which information is
received: formal and informal. Friends, neighbors, and
relatives--that is, personally known individuals--comprise the
informal, or interpersonal, channels. The formal channels
consist of all other sources of information: the mass media,
social agents and agencies, private enterprises--any commodity or activity in society, private or public, that is not related to individuals personally known to the receiver of information.

In one degree or another, channels of both types are
available to everyone in society, and everyone uses them
both. Is the nature of channel use different for the disadvantaged American?

Mostly, no. Somewhat, yes. Like others, the disadvantaged adult prefers to tap the informal network when he
needs a specific piece of information. For some subjects,
such as housing, grocery shopping, or job hunting, he may
prefer formal sources (163). When he does perceive a need
for information and opts to seek it, his search is often less
active (intense) than others (677).

On the other hand, the average adult is exposed to
great quantities of information that he does not actively seek
out for a specific problem of his own. Television, newspapers, magazines, films, and books provide a large portion
of this unsolicited information. The agents and agencies operating in society provide another part. The informal net-

work, friends, relatives, neighbors, provide still another.
Does he absorb all the information from these sources?
Of course not. We have very little hard knowledge about the
extent to which such unsolicited information is retained by the
individual. But we can be sure without doubt that not all of
it is. And based on the evidence of a few studies, we can
speculate that what a person knows is a function of the channels to which he is exposed, since some channels are richer
in information content than others. Typically, study after
study attributes high levels of informedness or awareness to
high levels of readership. People who read more know more.
They are more prepared to solve their problems.

It is true that the average American adult spends more
time with the electronic than with the print media. But is is
also true that the urban disadvantaged adult spends even more
of his time with the electronic media than the average adult.
Unlike his "average" counterpart, he relies on television to
the exclusion of other media, especially newspapers, magazines, and books, that are higher in information value (163).
And he puts more faith than the "average" adult in what television presents (247).

Warner has categorized information as either "ends"
information or "means" information--that which relates to
what you want to achieve, and that which relates to how to
achieve it. Ordinarily, the electronic media contain more
"ends" information; the print media, more "means" information (677, p. 3:30). Television, radio and movies provide information on commodities or life styles that can be striven
for; magazines, newspapers and books contain the information
that will help acquire the commodities or life styles that we
choose to strive for. Remembering that the disadvantaged
adult relies on the electronic media significantly more than

the average adult, we can see another way in which his information universe is circumscribed by his habits of media
use.   He is overexposed to "ends" information through television and radio, and sorely underexposed to the kind of information that might help him achieve the ends that he desires.

Again and again, studies point out that disadvantaged
people in general are significantly unaware of the social services that might be tapped for the solution of their problems
(for example, 138;181;629).   Not only are the names of the
agencies relatively unknown; so are the programs and responsibilities of the agencies.   On the other hand, where there
is "knowledge" of social helping programs, that knowledge
is frequently wrong: one investigation found that welfare
recipients consistently underestimate their own welfare entitlements and overestimate the welfare agent's authority (72).

Building on such data, some studies have found that
the strong non-print orientation of the disadvantaged adult is
a primary cause of his relatively greater ignorance of where
to turn.

There are indications, though, that seeking a solution
to a problem is very largely a matter of the intensity of the
felt need (373).   A few studies, particularly in the area of
employment, conclude that in certain situations the disadvantaged adult will turn to formal channels of information
more than the average adult.   This may spring from his
realization that the informal channels of communication to
which he has access are inadequate for his particular need.
The patterns of job-seeking, described above and again in
more detail in a later chapter, provide the best illustration
of this point.

The Impact of Information

The writings that deal with the impact of information
on the disadvantaged American present a picture of uncoordinated, scattered and tentative research whose results are
largely not comparable. It is tempting to speculate on impact
from the many surveys of expressed information need and
use, and channel use. However, there is no reason to assume that an expressed use of information is an actual use,
or that an expressed impact is an actual impact.

Without risking such assumptions, some assorted tentative observations on impact can be gleaned from the literature: A study of some CBS-TV programming concludes that
credibility of the information source is directly related to
the durability of impact (9). There is indication that among
ghetto populations 50 percent or more would use only commercial or in-ghetto sources or their own resources for information in problem solving (163).

Donohew and Singh report the conclusion that the innovator in the community is not necessarily exposed to the
mass media more than his non-innovating counterpart (173;
175). Yet Warner found that the respondents who were more
"successful" in solving their problems/questions were the
ones who (1) used more overall information sources, (2) used
personal contacts more, and (3) used magazines more as an
information source than the average (677). Voos reports on
a study of farmers indicating that the innovator, unlike the
"early adaptor, early majority, late majority and laggards, "
utilizes channels of information that transcend the community
(667).

There are suggestions that the purchasing behavior of
the urban black or white (not necessarily disadvantaged) is

influenced more by information from the white-oriented mass
media than by personal contacts (49). Voos asserts that
pragmatic information (i.e., comparative value) is not as
important in making purchase decisions as behavioristic in-
formation--color, scent, salesman, etc. (667). In some contrast, though, one consumer study has found that a shopper
with additional pragmatic information (a shopping list prepared
at home) spends $5 less per week on groceries than a shop-
per without that information (49).

It is uncertain what impact information has. Little
is known about:

> How the quality of life of the individual or community
> changes in the short or long term as the result of
> information
> The impact of information on individual and community
> demands on social and private service agencies
> How information affects actual decisions made
> How it affects the decision-making or problem-solving
> processes
> The relative impact of information from various chan-
> nels
> The relative importance of information in making deci-
> sions in various areas
> How forces within and around the individual influence
> him to act or not act on new information.

Portrait of the Disadvantaged American
in His Natural Information Habitat

The prototypal disadvantaged American, more than
his average counterpart:

> Does not know which formal channels to tap in order to
> solve his problems, or what specific programs ex-
> ist to respond to his needs
> Watches many hours of television daily, seldom reads
> newspapers and magazines and never reads books
> Does not see his problems as information needs
> Is not a very active information seeker, even when he
> does undertake a search
> May lean heavily on formal channels of information if

it becomes apparent that the informal channels are inadequate and if his need is strongly felt Is locked into an informal information network that is deficient in the information that is ordinarily available to the rest of society.

The most substantial overviews of communication, information, and the disadvantaged can be found in Block (49), Dervin (161), Dervin (163), Greenberg (245), Greenberg (247), Parker (484) and Warner (677).

IV

AREAS OF INFORMATION NEED

Health

GENERAL. Taken as a whole, the literature touching on the health-related information environment of the disadvantaged adult stresses four major problems:

1. The disadvantaged adults tend to know less about diseases--warning signals, symptoms, communicability, etc. --than adults with more education and income and higher social status (701;352). One study found that 46 percent of a sample of low socio-economic status adults with malignant cancer did not know the danger signs of cancer (701). And interestingly, while the aging adult becomes more and more concerned with his health, usually in response to overt signs of poorer health, he has been found to know less about health matters than his younger counterpart--even when controlling for education (73).

2. They tend not to know about preventive health services, such as pre-natal care, regular chest x-rays, dental care or health insurance (73;138;5;544;638;683). This trait is entirely consistent with the personal philosophies of most disadvantaged adults: fatalism, and a general unwillingness to delay gratification in favor of long-term benefits.

3. They tend not to know where to turn for health services in general, and they do not know which specific services are available (138;108). As with other topics, the informal network, friends, neighbors and relatives, is the

major channel through which health-related information is first sought.

4. Folk-medicine--both the formal kind, like shamanism, and the informal kind, like backwoods herbal pharmacology--is well entrenched among the non-urban disadvantaged, such as the Mexican-American, Eskimo, American Indian, and farm poor (147;202;453;352).

Cultural taboos, the perception of the body as competitive with the self, the cost of services, access to services, fear and simple ignorance--all these are barriers to the disadvantaged adult's search for health care information and health care. He will seek relief from health problems that are immediate, painful, and restrict his ability to perform his normal work.

We can find at least one writer who insists that merely broadcasting information will not affect the life of the disadvantaged man or woman. What is needed is a vigorous program of outreach (38). This does not necessarily preclude information-outreach, though. As another writer observes, the very shortage of health professionals in isolated rural areas (and, we would add, in urban ghettos) lends greater importance to a strong program of health education and information (199).

Health-related information needs intensify as we age. The literature seems to reflect this by spelling out information needs more clearly for the aging than for other groups of disadvantaged adults. The salient information needs for the aging center around:

1. heart problems
2. strokes
3. arthritis
4. medicare
5. podiatry

6. medical quackery (including drug quackery)
7. exercises
8. sex in old age
9. the physical changes that do and don't accompany
    old age (10;91;668;118)

A number of aspects of being aged stimulate needs in
these areas. The first aspect is simply that the body is old
and therefore susceptible to certain maladies--stroke, heart
problems, arthritis, skeletal problems, and others. The
second and third aspects, loneliness and poverty, conspire
to make older people especially easy marks for quacks and
hucksters who fill the empty hours with promises of a cheap
cure. And fourth, the aged resign themselves to poor health
in the mistaken belief that multitudes of ills and deficiencies
are a necessary part of growing older.

NUTRITION. A number of studies point out that nutritional deficiencies are common in the eating habits of
America's disadvantaged populations. Their diets are commonly lacking green and yellow vegetables, citric foods, and
dairy products (158;388;308). Yet differences do exist from
group to group. For instance, the Pueblo Indians in New
Mexico tend to lack meat protein in their diets (388). A
survey of the family diets of homemakers enrolled in a nutrition program indicated, although with little face validity,
that rural homemakers enjoy more nutritive diets than urban
homemakers (even though the former were more likely to
overlook the importance of meat protein); homemakers on
welfare have a stronger need for correction of their diets
than those not on welfare; black and Spanish respondents enjoy relatively better diets than the white respondents; users
of food stamps eat better than non-users of food stamps; the
better educated have fewer dietary lacks than the less educated (204).

The causes of nutritional deficiencies vary, and sometimes seem to contradict each other. Experts typically aver, usually on the basis of studies, that the disadvantaged are comparatively more ignorant of food and nutritive values than the general population (141;158;269;415;567). Along the same lines Cornely has discovered a widespread acceptance of nutritional myths such as "milk and fish, if eaten together, will make you sick" (140;141). This seems to be especially true among the less educated and black segments of a predominately low-income urban sample.

Lack of information can be a function of communication patterns. For instance, Massoth and Alexander insist that groups such as migrant workers and American Indians are not served well by nutritional guides written in the language of middle-class, white America (415;6). Poor nutrition may be related not only to the absence of information, as most experts tend to suggest, but also to the way in which that information is communicated or received. Further, many experts suggest that the problem does not hinge on information per se. There is the suggestion that lack of money is a root cause of malnutrition among the aging poor (697).

Also, a specific culture can impose dietary norms that are not necessarily nutritious (415). For instance, Florida migrant workers spend their "extra" food money on meat rather than on food that would balance their diet (158). The isolation of the aging poor can result in malnutrition (158); dietary deficiencies tend to disappear when group dining is practiced[1] (123).

It is commonly held that even the disadvantaged sectors of society view proper nutrition as important. And one study found that the basis of poor nutrition among a sample of Louisiana low-income families was not so much ignorance

of which foods were necessary for good health as it was a
lack of motivation to practice what they already knew (330).

The many studies and sermons related to nutrition indicate a need for several kinds of information:

1. The nutritive values of foods
2. How to plan nutritious meals
3. How to prepare tasty, nutritious dishes
4. How to capitalize on available foods for a nutritious
   diet (this includes the use of donated foods, sea-
   sonal and locally abundant food sources)
5. Adequate diets for different age groups
6. The use of the Food Stamp Donated Food Program
   of the Department of Agriculture
7. Best buys in nutritious food
8. Misinformation and faddism about foods
9. The common nutritional problems, such as obesity
   and malnutrition, and their prevention
10. Minimum daily requirements of vitamins and min-
    erals (especially of interest to the elderly).

FAMILY PLANNING. Considerable social energy is
currently being directed toward controlling the size of fam-
ilies--that is, toward giving parents and potential parents the
predispositions and means to keep their family size within
the limits that they desire.

Judging from some reports, this energy is being directed toward the proper target. Poor non-white mothers,
disadvantaged by virtue of race and economic level, claim
that they want fewer children than white mothers claim; yet
they consistently bear more (320;533). One study even indicates that poor undereducated mothers have about twice as
many children as they would like to have (137). It is specu-
lated that the primary benefits accruing from the ability to
plan family size are improved health, increased per capita
income, and greater manageability of the family (29).

There are many facets to providing "predispositions
and means." Birth control technology, attitudes toward

family planning and knowledge of technology, human physiology and related services are all part of the picture.

"Low utilization or motivation may be the reason for
the contraceptive failures rather than lack of knowledge" (601).
The bulk of the documents examined acknowledge the importance of information in achieving widespread family planning
among the disadvantaged. Nonetheless, the documents taken
together allow no other conclusion except that lack of information in and of itself is not the major barrier to sweep-
ing social change. Instead, it is fear, legal restriction, cultural taboo, religious proscription, poor self-image and limited world view that emerge from the literature as the critical barriers to the acceptance and practice of family planning.

Disadvantaged women, more than the average, fear the
side effects of such contraceptives as the pill (153). Too,
they are more likely than the average woman to feel important only when pregnant; as an extreme example, the American Indian woman generally feels worthless if she cannot
bear children (153;178).

In some subcultures the man's objection or potential
objection to birth control exerts a strong influence against
the use of contraceptives by the woman. The Mexican-American man has a particularly strong machismo and tends to
feel extraordinarily potent when his woman is pregnant (243).

The disadvantaged are especially reluctant to dis-
cuss sex, husband-to-wife (153).

The poor in general--and in one study the Appalachian
poor in particular--adhere to a fatalistic view of life. The
idea of family planning is not consistent with this view (533;
495).

There are instances where _formal_ social codes in-
hibit the practice of birth control. For instance, in New

York City before 1964, only M.D.'s could make family planning referrals, and then only when the patient's health was
in danger (182). The preconceptions of clinic workers have
also been seen as barriers to the spread of family planning.
One study found that they consistently underestimated the degree to which the poor would actually read a booklet on family planning (53).

     These are not barriers of information per se. They
will not dissolve simply with the distribution of more information. Rather, they call for changes in attitudes, cultural
norms and legal codes.

     There are studies that support the contention that in-
formation alone is not the key to disseminating the practice
of family planning. A number of investigators indicate that
the knowledge of at least one effective method of contracep-
tion is common among various disadvantaged groups, from
Appalachia to Hawaii. A study in New York and one in
Hawaii each found that 83 percent of the respondents had theo-
retical knowledge adequate for effective use of at least one
contraceptive. A second New York study found that 89 percent of the respondents knew where to turn for professional
information on birth control (683;713;601;658). These findings
are seemingly contradicted by a study of New Orleans black
women, which concluded that a lack of birth control information prevailed among them. However, those respondents were
tested on their knowledge of reproductive physiology, rather
than just on their knowledge of birth control per se. And
while we might make the assumption that the two are closely
related, the author's conclusions strain the assumption, especially in light of the other contradictory conclusions.

     Still, there is a body of literature that points to the
need for information. Low-income, hospitalized New Yorkers

were asked "Do you think most people know enough about
birth control information?"; 92 percent claimed that most
people do not (601). Two-thirds of the aides working in the
Expanded Food and Nutrition Education Program throughout
the fifty states said that two-thirds of their female clients
ask for birth control information; and 94 percent said their
clients needed that kind of information (71). Among the Appalachian poor, even though the prevailing Protestant funda-
mentalism is a powerful barrier to the practice of family
planning, ignorance of where to go for information is an even
more effective barrier (230). It seems, then, that while
some knowledge of birth control and family planning pervades
society and even reaches the disadvantaged, there is a need
for more information.

There is indication, too, that knowledge is distributed
non-randomly, even at the disadvantaged end of the social
continuum. As with most topics, knowledge about family
planning is greatest among those who are more educated,
have larger incomes, are white, active (in this case, prac-
ticers of birth control) and knowledgeable about other things.

Where information needs do exist, they tend to revolve
around the following:

1. The practicability of family planning; prerequisite
to changing attitudes is the knowledge that family planning
is possible (318).

2. The reliability of the various birth control methods
(54); inherent in this is the dispelling of certain myths of
birth control such as "Female orgasm is necessary for con-
ception" or "Urination after intercourse is a form of con-
traception" (601).

3. The possible dangers and side effects of each
method.

4. The technique of application of the various methods.

    5. The existence of birth control clinics; in a Nash-
ville study, only one-half of the low income women in public housing knew a clinic existed (318).

    6. Where contraceptives are prescribed.

    7. Where contraceptives can be procured; items 6
and 7 are often confused (713).

As important as the information itself is the way in
which it is delivered. Most important, family planning should
not be presented as a threat to current lifestyles, but as an
enrichment, both now and in old age. In addition, information should be directed to men as well as women, for the influence of men in the acceptance and regular practice of
birth control is considerable (42).

ABORTION. The abortion picture in America has
changed rapidly in recent years. A number of state legisla-
tures and courts, as well as a recent decision of the U.S.
Supreme Court, have begun establishing abortion as a human
right. This will have untold ramifications for the information atmosphere that surrounds the topic. Some changes have
begun to occur already.

Studies have indicated that, to date, word-of-mouth
through friends has been the common way of transmitting information about obtaining abortions (33). It has been the
same channel through which other information about abortion
has been communicated--its advantages, risks, costs and
procedures. As a result of the changes in the ethos, the
channels of communication of this topic should become more
open, and more formal. Already new counseling, information and referral services have sprung up. They have often
been advertised prominently on large billboards in urban
areas. And, while social discriminations against the disadvantaged woman--especially the poor woman--will still
cause her to ask "Where can I get an illegal abortion?"

(260), other questions will become increasingly frequent:

    1. Biological: Is it dangerous? Can I have children at a later time?

    2. Legal: At what age does the fetus become protected by law? Must I defend an abortion on the basis of health? Economic duress? Damage to the fetus? Am I liable under the law?

    3. Directional: Who is a trustworthy abortionist? When can I see him? Where is he located?

    4. Financial: How much will it cost? Is there a free service?

    5. Counseling: What will my husband and family think? How will I feel afterward? Should I go ahead and have the baby?

VENEREAL DISEASE. Few documents deal with adult information needs in the area of venereal disease; teenagers are the focal group more often than not. If we assume that the younger adults share the problem with their adolescent counterparts, though, we might draw some tentative conclusions from existing documents.

Knowledge of venereal disease is incomplete and distorted, particularly among the lower socio-economic groups. Poor education and broken homes foster a knowledge gap on the subject itself and on where to turn for information and help (164;165). While the available literature doesn't specify the gaps, we could posit some needs for information:

1. How to detect VD in oneself and in others
2. How to prevent VD in oneself
3. How to stop the spread of VD among one's peers
4. Where to turn for preventive technology
5. Where to turn for cures
6. Where to turn for psychological counseling with regard to VD.

As with most information needs, the ones above fall into the broad categories: kinetic and potential. The bulk of social hope in the area of VD is founded on satisfying

potential information needs--preparing the individual with information before an emergency arises--so that there will be
fewer kinetic needs, fewer emergencies.

DRUG ABUSE AND ALCOHOLISM. "The role of facts
in determining use of harmful drugs is unclear. ... [I]nfor-
mation levels have not been shown to play a dominant role
among the factors related to different forms of drug use"
(263, p.1337-8). A number of writers support this assertion (289;195). One speculates that if information holds any
power to dissuade youths from using harmful drugs, it is information on the forces that motivate drug use, not information on the dangers of drugs alone (315). One writer contra-
dicts the general pattern by concluding that there was a significant drop in the use of LSD in 1966-8 due to the availability of factual information (151).

While there are pleas for drug information that is
more accurate and more relevant to the background of the
potential receiver, the documents examined reveal nothing
more specific about the information needed.

Almost no literature deals with information, alcoholism and the disadvantaged. In two studies of the information
needs of Sioux and Navajo Indian tribes, though, it was found
that information related to alcoholism and drug abuse was
consistently valued more than information on communicable
diseases and venereal disease (449;450).

MENTAL HEALTH. Discussions of the disadvantaged
adult's information needs in the area of mental health are
few. What relevant literature there is characterizes the disadvantaged adult as one suffering from inadequate referral
services and lacking information on (1) mental health services available and (2) the characteristics of mental health
problems (185;249). In contrast, a few studies indicate that

there is a sizeable need to know in this area, measured both
by the kinds and number of queries received at mental health
clinics and by the extent of mental health problems among
low-income families (625;249). One study somewhat contra-
dicts such conclusions. Lilienfeld found that lower-class
patients of a mental health clinic were much more knowledgeable, fearless, sensitive, realistic and tolerant in the area
of mental health than the professional's stereotyped view of
them would admit (380).

Despite this contradiction, though, the literature strongly supports the assertion that the major problem in delivering
mental health care services is not information, per se, but
a combination of the predispositions of the clients in seeking
and following advice, and the actual performance of the service agencies that exist.

SICKLE CELL ANEMIA. Although we launched a pur-
poseful search for documents that would shed light on information needs related to sickle cell anemia, none was found.

Home and Family

(Some aspects of home and family, such as health, consumer-
ism, housing, nutrition and education are treated separately
elsewhere.)

Home and family are often mentioned in documents
dealing with life patterns and needs. The disadvantaged
American is generally viewed as a poorer than average house-
keeper, although he does not generally perceive a serious
need for help in improving his houskeeping, and a poor plan-
ner and budgeter. His relations with others in the family
are seen as deficient: he lacks the understanding to raise
children well, even though he perceives it to be of paramount

importance, or to sustain a successful relationship with his
spouse.   More than the average, one parent has left the
family.

The solutions typically proposed center around education of some kind: learn how to manage money, plan meals,
prepare food, store food, care for babies, understand ado-
lescents, mend and alter clothes, clean the house, repair
the house, keep the house safe; adopt a new attitude toward
sanitation in the kitchen; understand the importance of planning tasty meals (254; 285; 303; 305; 343).   There are cases where
public housing authorities require "below-par" housekeepers
to attend classes on child care, family relations, meal planning and budgeting (117).

Invariably, the solution to home and family problems
is something that needs to be learned, an attitude that needs
to be changed, or a habit that needs to be reformed.   Rarely
is information seen as a cure.   That is, while there are
certainly needs for discrete pieces of information that focus
on home and family, few of these needs are expressed in the
literature on disadvantaged populations, perhaps because most
of the questions that need answering are not unique to the
disadvantaged home and family.   Yet the literature allows us
to construct a few prototype questions that might illustrate
some of the special information needs of the disadvantaged
adult.

How do I get my baby into a day care center?
Whom do I talk to to get rid of rats?
My husband walked out on me three weeks ago.   What do
    I do?
How do I know if I have lead-based paint on the walls?
Where can I get $10 to last till my welfare check comes
    in?
I need enough food to get us through the weekend.
How do I get an abandoned car removed from in front of
    my house?

There's a gang of kids terrorizing the neighborhood.
Where do I turn?
My daughter has been acting funny lately. Can anyone
  help?

While the disadvantaged adult may have a great need
for such information, his need for learning, especially in the
areas of child care, housekeeping and budgeting, is greater,
possibly because he does not possess the machinery (skills,
talents, stored knowledge, attitudes, awareness) necessary to
deal with the raw materials, or information. The primary
need, as the literature continually emphasizes, is for the development of the disadvantaged adult's cognitive and affective
machinery. For the most part, he has new skills to learn
and new attitudes to adopt before pure information will serve
him in the area of home and family.

Consumer Affairs

A composite view of the disadvantaged adult as a consumer begins to materialize through the literature.

He gives less attention to product quality than the
average adult (609).

He has great gaps in what he knows, when compared
with the general population. He appears to be gullible
(40).

He tends to distrust small ghetto merchants, unless
they share his ethnic background. This is especially the
case with blacks (491;41).

The urban ghetto resident, while to some extent locked
into local shopping, may be more mobile and, therefore,
more able to exercise choice in buying than some writers
claim (608;633;41). In support of this, it has been found
that location of the merchant is only the third priority fac-
tor in making purchase choices (41).

Although a study of blacks in the Watts area of Los
Angeles is contradictory, a number of studies indicate that
the disadvantaged adult does not typically rank consumer

information high on a list of priorities, despite glaring gaps
in his knowledge (126;655;450;449;677).   Because of limited
financial resources, he is inordinately reliant on credit buying, for major purchases.   This is the heart of most of his
consumer problems (331).

He is often at the mercy of the seller.   For instance,
the National Commission on Civil Disorders reported that in
twenty states the wages of a buyer can be diverted to a cred-
itor merely upon the latter's deposition, with no prior opportunity for the buyer to forestall the action.   In Washington,
D. C., it was found that this was happening to one out of
every eleven low-income purchasers of furniture and appli-
ances (655).

He does not rely on personal channels as much for
consumer information as he does for other kinds of information (46;529).   For consumer information he is likely to regard newspapers more highly than television (48).   If he has
more formal education, he is more likely to rely on print
media over broadcast media for his consumer information
and more likely to make choices based on cost rather than
convenience (47).   While the high TV user tends to possess
certain low-level kinds of consumer information (especially
awareness of information sources), the print user is in control of more exact and useable information, such as what
specific kinds of information are available to him (161).

If he is a disadvantaged urban black he is more likely
to be an informed consumer than if he is a disadvantaged
urban white (100).   He is subject to an almost endless variety
of fraudulent practices (442;477;558;641):

    "bait-and-switch"
    signing blank contracts
    "free" gifts
    billing errors

non-receipt of mail-order goods
hidden interest charges
"credit investigation" fees
excessive service charges
"confession of judgment, " whereby the buyer agrees that
    all the unpaid balance falls due immediately if one
    payment is missed
referral schemes (collusion among merchants)
the raising of prices on selected items on days when wel-
    fare checks and food stamps are issued
the "pyramid" sales scheme, a kind of commercial chain
    letter that promises to make the buyer rich if he
    can recruit other buyers.

He lacks understanding of some basic consumer concepts: he does not understand the game of comparison shopping and unit pricing. He cannot interpret the information on
product labels. The concepts of collateral and mortgage financing are complicated mysteries. He doesn't know how to
handle door-to-door salesmen, and he is not disposed to budgeting, especially where long term planning is required.

Voos asserts that the consumer is essentially in need
of three kinds of information: marketer-dominated, consumer-dominated, and neutral (667). The environment of the
disadvantaged person is relatively rich in marketer-dominated
information and deficient in consumer-dominated and neutral
information. He tends not to turn to his personal channels
of consumer-dominated information--friends, relatives, neigh-
bors--and the generally formal sources of neutral information, such as Consumer Reports, as often as he turns to information that is controlled by the marketer. His buying information comes primarily from face-to-face contact with the
merchant or from the merchant's television or newspaper ad-
vertisements.

A number of rather specific information needs, some
closely tied to legal problems, can be identified through the
literature in the areas of:

Term purchasing
        interest rates; the difference between credit price
           and real price
        buyer liabilities, such as garnishment of salary,
           reclaiming merchandise, punitive legal action
        mortgage financing
Protection
        where to go with a grievance
        prevailing consumer protection laws
Shopping
        brands
        prices
        guarantees of performance
        service contracts
Dealers
        reliability
        service record
        location.

Housing

However you describe it--need, problem, lack, area of interest, or subject of inquiry--housing is the most consistently high-ranking concern to the disadvantaged. In the King County, Washington, legal service program, applications for aid in the area of tenant-landlord problems ranks third in frequency (532). It is second in number of problems dealt with in one Community Action Program and in the frequency of queries received by the Model Cities Community Information Center of Philadelphia (194;350). In two other studies, the American Indian and the aging identify decent housing as their major concern (717;123). There is a small body of evidence indicating that housing problems are more critical among the disadvantaged than among the population as a whole. Warner and others, reporting on a study of the information needs of a large sample in the Baltimore area, found that while the general population ranked housing as third most critical, the non-white and low-income indicated

that it was their most critical problem/question (677).
The literature offers a little evidence in partial explanation, perhaps, of this obsession with housing matters. While it does not account for the total phenomenon, it does light the way to some understanding of the atmosphere that exacerbates the housing problems of the disadvantaged:

> Housing professionals--brokers, agents--cannot make a reasonable profit from serving the poor, and are therefore reluctant to do so (253).

> Low income families are incapable of bargaining for units that are available (654).

> The poor man locates in response to crisis. He will often wait to seek help until after he has been evicted (253;623).

> Certain ethnic groups (for example, blacks) may find the housing market closed to them even though they have the money to buy (300).

> The aging tend to be resigned to their present dwellings, even though inadequate; when they seek help in relocating, they tend not to pursue that help for very long before becoming resigned again and giving up the search (517).

> In addition, the aging individual is particularly subject to fraudulent practices in housing; for example, untruthful promotion of retirement lots (472).

> The disadvantaged adult is consistently characterized as being ignorant of the housing available, his tenant rights and entitlements, the costs of housing and home financing, and his responsibilities as a tenant or homeowner (253;235).

> He is generally unaware of redevelopment planning which may eventually necessitate his relocating. He learns that he must relocate only after plans have been _formally_ approved (253).

> He tends not to know where to go for help in purchasing homes. For instance, only 50 percent of the white and 30 percent of the black rural poor know of the existence of the Farmer's Home Administration, and even fewer know of its specific programs for aid to the prospective homeowner (181).

He knows less often than the general population where
to take grievances. It has been found that the more socially handicapped (lower status) tenants of public housing
were more ignorant of who was responsible for housing
matters. For instance, they saw the project manager
rather than the housing authority board as the rule-maker
(372).

The disadvantaged adult, like others in the society, is
a tenant or a homeowner, a prospective home buyer or a prospective renter. Like others, too, he is a relocator--some-
one in search of new housing. Unlike others, though, he
often relocates under duress, as the result of urban redevelopment. In all of these roles, he has information needs
that can be identified. Most of them hold for the advantaged
populations as well; some few uniquely or predominantly per-
tain to the disadvantaged subcultures. There are three broad
areas of information need: finding, funding, and dwelling.

Finding: Where are rental units and sales units located, by price? (Including homes for the ages.) What
social agencies or professional enterprises can help locate
housing? Where can temporary living quarters be found for
a recent immigrant? What kind of record does each landlord have in the area of tenant relations? An even broader
panorama of questions is associated with finding adequate
housing in a new area: What social and medical services
are available, and where? What are the public transportation patterns? What jobs are available? Are the public
schools nearby? What are they like? Is it a safe neighborhood? Are city services adequate? Most of these and other
questions related to relocation are dealt with in other parts
of this book.

Funding: What subsidies or subsidized housing are
available? (This includes public housing and cash grants for
housing.) What are the entitlements of the individual, and

what are the eligibility requirements? What are the hidden
costs of buying, especially for first-time buyers? (30). The
hidden costs of renting? Is there any reimbursement of
moving expenses for those who are forced to relocate? Or
a bonus for finding their own new housing? (84).

Dwelling: What are the rights of the individual in
cases of harassment, eviction, or non-compliance of the landlord with the leasing agreement? (286). What are the pro-
visions for rent regulation and code enforcement? (194).
What are the limits of rent-withholding by the tenant? (150).
What are the responsibilities of the locality to the renter or
homeowner? (Streets, sewage, water, etc.) What, in turn,
are the renters' and homeowners' liabilities? Where does
the individual turn with grievances on any of these matters?

The sources of these various kinds of information are
diverse: builders' associations, banks and other lending
agencies, real estate boards, apartment and mobile home
associations, neighborhood associations, local, national and
state social service agencies, census data, human rights
commissions, and the U.S. Postal Service, among others
(300). Perhaps it is the very diversity of sources of information (and, consequently, control) that precipitates the need
for better coordination among them. A buyer who was grant-
ed an FHA mortgage on a house that did not meet local
standards--that is, a condemned house--might have been pro-
tected if the information emanating from the FHA and the
local authorities had been properly orchestrated (422).

In addition, residents of urban ghettos, especially,
need to be continually informed about areas that are being
considered for redevelopment in order to preclude panic as
the result of rumor and to allow them to plan their own relocation.

Employment

The topic of employment has stimulated the richest literature related to the information needs of disadvantaged
adults. Many studies have accumulated over the past ten
years. They focus primarily on the urban or newly urban
male and allow some comparison between black and white,
skilled and unskilled, poor and not-so-poor.
With few exceptions (95) it is conceded or assumed
that the disadvantaged adult suffers from a lack of job information and that this in turn hinders his efforts at job
seeking. In one of the rare studies of affective behavioral
change resulting from information, Stevens concluded that increased job information leads to both increased job seeking
activity and to greater success at actually securing a job
(604).

The kinds of information need can be broadly classi-
fied as:

1. Generalizations on the job market--local, regional,
   and national, short term and long term--for the purposes of planning job search and training activities
2. Specific jobs available--local, regional, and national
3. Qualifications for those jobs--skills, education, etc.
4. Wages and fringe benefits of the jobs
5. Available transportation[2]
6. Job training and retraining opportunities--location,
   nature, requirements, prerequisites, cost.

A standard list of job information sources can be
drawn from the literature. The formal sources are: public
employment services, private employment services, unions
and newspaper want ads. The informal: friends, relatives
and neighbors, direct inquiry at the employer's door, and
(occasionally) street corners.

There are a number of contradictory findings about
job-related information seeking behavior--contradictory pos-

sibly because of varying definitions and unequatable populations.   Taken together, though, the results provide a relatively consistent picture of job information seeking behavior,
probably best represented by a lengthy quote from Lurie and
Rayack's report on their study of blue collar workers.   Until their research has been replicated on the various disadvantaged groups, we might hypothesize (and other reports
centering on the disadvantaged support the hypothesis) that
the following observations on the Negro population are generalizable in some degree to all groups that are locked out
of the dominant middle-class culture.   Even the ghettoized,
poor, low-occupation white person can be expected to suffer
similar cultural controls and to behave in a similar manner,
although the white person would likely be slightly more print-
oriented than the black person, all other things being equal.

> The relatively poor employment record of Negroes
> may be explained in part by the less adequate
> sources of job information--in terms of both num-
> ber and quality of sources--available to them than
> to whites of comparable skill.   Our research shows
> that most jobs are obtained by workers of both
> races using informal methods of job search--direct
> plant application and information obtained from rela-
> tives and friends.   Informal search, however, op-
> erates more effectively for white workers since
> their friends and relatives are already integrated
> within all levels of the occupational structure.   The
> contacts that the job-seeking Negro must rely upon
> are, on the other hand, concentrated in the poorer-
> paying, less desirable occupations.   The dependence
> of Negroes upon the kind of information available
> from friends or relatives tends to perpetuate the
> existing patterns of employment.   Furthermore, in
> making direct application to plants, Negroes will
> tend to go to those firms where they have reason
> to believe there are 'Negro jobs.'

> To break out of these existing patterns and find
> employment higher up on the occupational ladder,
> the Negro must turn to institutional intermediaries.

However, these intermediaries, as they now function, do not hold out much hope for him. He gets
relatively little assistance from private employment
services and practically none from unions--both
sources of information for many of the better pay-
ing jobs--and he also seems reluctant to use want-
ads.

Since Negroes get little help from private institutional intermediaries, they are compelled to rely
much more heavily than whites on the public employment service. Unfortunately, state employment
services, as they are now organized and operating
--even in the North--do little more than maintain
existing discriminatory patterns, for the budgets
of the state employment services depend largely on
the number of placements. Therefore, the Negro
job-seeker is likely to be referred to jobs where
there is little chance of rejection, i. e., to 'Negro
jobs' [395, p. 92].

It should be noted that in other studies (e. g., 677)
newspaper want ads are fairly consistently described as a
little used source of information.

On the subject of job training: the sole significant
report concluded that the disadvantaged urban adult is generally uninformed and unenthusiastic about job training opportunities. It went on to state that black adults were less informed and less enthusiastic than others in the sample (95).
The findings are congruent with the ignorance and fatalistic
outlook that seem to infest the psyche and behavior of the
most disadvantaged groups. No document dealt with the
disadvantaged adult's information needs on the job.

Welfare Programs

(For our purposes they include public assistance checks,
veterans' benefits, social security, Medicare and Medicaid,
food stamps, Aid to Families with Dependent Children, surplus food programs, free school lunches, public and subsidized housing.)

In his classic study of information and referral processes related to social service, Alfred Kahn has written, "There is evidence that users of the entire social welfare network are less adequately served because of defects at the 'doorway' and in information services" (335, p. 58).

The disadvantaged American in need of welfare assistance is faced with a maze of agencies. Each of them dispenses a variety of social goods. As a whole, they hand out a wide array of commodities or services--welfare checks, surplus food, day care for the children, family counseling, etc. From the individual's vantage point the welfare system is a jungle of poorly defined agencies that compete with and sometimes contradict each other. They come wrapped in red tape and restrictions that are designed to confuse him or render the "assistance" useless. They seem to be designed more to regulate his life than to make it better.

The welfare recipient sees the benefits as privileges, not rights. If asked, he will probably be more certain of the agency's rights than of his own, and more certain of his obligations to the agency than of the agency's obligations to him (72). He may, though, be "certain" of misinformation. For instance, he may harbor an unfounded fear that a lien will be attached to all his property if he applies for welfare (181).

In the face of such chaos, what are the individual's information needs? Basically they are:

1. Which programs are available to fit his needs?

2. How do two or more welfare programs interrelate? (For example, Medicare and Medicaid; or Social Security, public assistance and veteran's benefits.) Which combinations are allowed? Which will provide the greatest benefits?

3. What are the eligibility requirements and his continuing obligations?

4. How does he apply for a welfare benefit?

5. How can he appeal a decision to deny assistance or withdraw benefits?

What makes these needs so problematic is the bewildering complexity of the welfare system itself, the gross, uncoordinated welter of activities that has evolved apparently without plan and seems to do nothing quite so well as confuse the needy and keep him from his rightful benefits. Some welfare agencies--notably, the Social Security Administration--have recognized the situation and have attempted to rectify it. They have adopted referral or switching activities to help get the client to the proper social agency. By and large, though, referral activities have been adopted reluctantly. The agencies do not see them as part of their service mission. (For an example, see the discussion of referral activities in the Social Security Administration, 257.)

At this point the dissemination of information among the various welfare programs and from the programs to the potential clients is still chaotic. Thus, the information needs of the disadvantaged adult in pursuit of welfare benefits-- needs which otherwise would be fairly straightforward and obvious--are complicated.

As with most subject areas, a potential client is more likely to know where to go for a welfare benefit if he (1) has a higher level of general knowledge, (2) has a more critical felt need for it, (3) feels more in control of the course of his own life and (4) engages in more social interaction (435).

Law

"Even if the poor are not hostile to lawyers, there is no assurance that they will seek out legal help when they need it, or even that they have the knowledge to discern a need for legal counsel" (543, p. 4).

For most disadvantaged groups, this quotation describes two of the three primary barriers to seeking legal help: first, the tendency not to see a problem as having legal ramifications; second, the widespread apathy or downright hostility toward the formal legal services that are available. The disadvantaged adult's problems begin here, with an at best neutral attitude toward the social agencies that dispense legal information and advice, and an inability to perceive a specific personal situation as one requiring legal information or advice.

Lack of information is the third barrier. Although information per se is certainly not the only root cause of legal problems of the disadvantaged, it is of some importance. There is widespread ignorance of what legal services, both professional and para-professional, are available--which agencies will provide help on which specific problems, which lawyers will take which kinds of cases, where free legal advice can be gotten, etc.

Within this general information barrier that separates the disadvantaged American from legal service, we can identify moments when legal information may be important. The need for specific pieces of legal information can pervade all areas of everyone's life. Virtually every other topic we deal with in these pages has its legal aspect, and the individual has a potential set of legal information needs related to each.

To illustrate the extent to which legal information needs infest every aspect of daily life, a list of problems with legal ramifications has been extracted from the literature dealing with the disadvantaged. While few of the topics are unique to the disadvantaged American, the texture of the whole list emphasizes more the concerns of the disadvantaged than those of the general American population.

Consumer products; advertising frauds
Contract liability: warranties, service pacts, mort-
gages, etc. (including treaty rights of American
Indians)
Credit financing; borrowing
Bill collecting; garnishment of salary
Bankruptcy
Workmen's compensation
Job security
Landlord vs. tenant: eviction, rent raise, withholding
rent, violations of housing codes or leases
Relocation due to urban renewal or public construction
Welfare entitlements: medical care, financial assist-
ance, food stamps, public day care, etc.
Arrests (especially, right to counsel before hearings
in the case of a misdemeanor, 233)
Bail
Trial, including undue postponement of trial and right
to court-appointed counsel
Criminal records
Appeal of convictions (one report, 688, advocates "le-
gal checkups" for convicted persons, so that their
cases can be reviewed in the light of relevant new
laws and court decisions)
Probation
Commitment to mental institutions
Torts (slander, libel and other wrongful actions that
are not a misdemeanor)
Automobile and domestic liabilities
Divorce, separation, annulment, non-support
Adoption, guardianship, child custody, paternity
Death and burial
Estate, wills and probate
Infringement of human rights (for example, racial and
ethnic discrimination or illegal search and seizure).

The literature points out a few areas in which the disadvantaged adult, particularly in urban areas, can be expected
to have a more pressing need than the average citizen: consumer fraud, tenant rights, welfare entitlements and civil
(human) rights, especially in the period between arrest and
first court appearance (104;685).

The documents examined make several areas of legal
concern conspicuous by their absence: securities and bonds,

and taxation. This lack cannot be taken as a representation of reality. It cannot be assumed with certainty that an individual will not have an information need in these areas just because he is "disadvantaged." Recent social programs aimed at promoting private enterprise among the urban disadvantaged are enough evidence of a need for information related to corporate law and taxation. The lack of any mention of these topics illustrates how stereotypes persist even in the literature that is responsible for reforming stereotypes into realistic generalizations.

The Political Process

>"While most resources provided by a public
>information utility will work to the benefit of
>those already possessed of political resources,
>this need not completely be the case. Per-
>sons presently disfranchised or penalized by
>lack of information can, with respect to cer-
>tain types of information, redress their dis-
>advantage. In this respect, the information
>system can lead to more equitable distribu-
>tion of resources" (510, p. 294-5).

While there is little empirical evidence about public knowledge of the political process,[3] it is widely acknowledged that the general population has only limited access to and/or control of information related to local, state, and federal government and law enforcement. There is widespread ignorance of actions pending and actions taken, of the processes of legislation, administration, adjudication and law enforcement, of the distribution of power locally, nationally and in between, and of where to go to find out about these things.

Two reports, on Spanish and black citizens in the Miami-Dade County area and on black ghetto-dwellers in other cities, provide some very limited evidence that disadvantaged urban Americans are inordinately lacking in information on the political process[4] (34;655).

Part of the answer may be found in the reluctance of
the disadvantaged (in one case, Mexican-Americans in Los
Angeles) to take their grievances to formally designated
agencies (419). It is possible that the disadvantaged are not
accustomed to dealing with complex systems of role behavior
such as those found in bureaucratic service agencies (372).
Thus, their access to potentially valuable sources of information is curtailed.

The literature makes a strong plea for adequate down-
ward communication. But it pleads even more urgently for
two-way vertical communication--a continuing dialogue between the little man at the bottom and the complex, often in-
sensitive governmental and law enforcement machinery at the
top. One report calls for the establishment of "neighborhood
city halls"; another advocates a public information utility that
makes use of computer and cable television technologies;
still another proposes a citizen's panel to serve as a barometer of community processes and to communicate with the
politicians who control the allocation of resources (655;459;
326). Several writers argue for the services of a local ombudsman to help interpret the political process for the citizen and communicate the citizen's needs upward to governmental authorities.

A preliminary checklist of kinds of information needs
in the area of the political process can be extracted from
the literature:

> Watchdog information on action pending and action taken
>   that affect the community
> Where to go to complain, to ask, or to suggest
> Crisis information in times of civil disorder (rumor
>   control)
> The performance records of politicians and public ser-
>   vants

Information on the status and changes in the community: population changes, redevelopment plans and
activities, community health and safety, education,
and property values and ownership (88;243;655;326).

It would be misleading to represent these broad needs
as the needs of disadvantaged Americans alone. It appears
that virtually every citizen lacks the information through
which he could begin to control his destiny within the political
process. Yet it may be that, once again, the disadvantaged
citizen has a more intense need, since he is less knowledgeable to begin with.

Transportation

"The Watts experiment, while not a full test
of the precise extent to which employment of
slum residents can be increased through better transportation links, shows that employment does increase as transportation difficulties are removed" (475, p. 77).

One of the major transportation difficulties, according
to the writer above, is the inadequacy of the related information. Others conclude from their studies of general adult
needs that transportation ranks relatively low (49;121). The
importance of the problem does increase for those who live
in sparsely settled areas that are almost totally lacking in
public transportation facilities.

To the extent that transportation is a matter of concern, though, it is somewhat of an information problem.
The small amount of literature that touches on the information deficiencies surrounding transportation deals only with
public transportation. It stresses the inadequacies of time-
tables and route maps (too confusing in their completeness or
too uninformative in their incompleteness), transportation
personnel (too impatient with the aged and handicapped), and

entrance, exit and passageway signs (infrequent, poorly light-
ed, printed too small, equivocal) (98;229;475;700).

Only two substantial documents came to the surface:
Ornati and others evaluate the public transportation information available in the New York and Los Angeles metropolitan
areas. They make very specific recommendations for improving the information available to the low-income New Yorker,
such as providing a map of the complete transit system, including all public and private bus routes, rapid transit routes,
major terminals, and street background. They urge that the
map be distributed free at agencies concerned with employment in poverty areas (475).

Leonard and Newman report on some experimentation
with four methods of instructing blind persons in the use of
new pedestrian routes. They conclude that either a hand-
held braille disc, an audio tape, or a spatial diagram are
superior to verbal instructions-plus-memory in getting the
blind person from point A to point B. They point out, though,
that in addition to improvements such as those mentioned
above, phones in passageways, varying floor textures and
pulsed non-verbal signals could all be employed to facilitate
the blind person's use of public transportation systems (368).

Education

The literature on the subject of education, remedial
education, adult education and vocational education related to
the various disadvantaged groups is great. However, since
our avowed purpose was to seek out not the educational needs,
but the informational ones, we limited our scope within this
broad area to information needs about education and educational opportunities. Our search criteria rejected documents

that dealt exclusively with the content of educational programs.
Instead, we retrieved material on how information about educational programs is sought, how that information is used,
and what additional information might be needed.

Under this limitation, the number of document "hits"
approached zero. But even though the documents in the
chosen area are very few, some tentative observations can
be advanced.

The disadvantaged adult places a high value on general and diverse education for his children (even though his
expectation of his child's success varies from group to group).
However, he is not disposed to pursue his own formal learning if he does not see that immediate, almost tangible, results will accrue. He ranks his own need for education well
below his need to earn a living (485;638;677). A great bulk
of the literature stresses the urgency of motivating the individual to undertake some form of education.

As far as learning about educational opportunities,
the literature indicates that invariably the disadvantaged person learns about adult educational programs through informal
contacts--friends, neighbors, relatives. While the media
may reinforce the informal contacts, their effectiveness in
recruiting is questionable (273;57).

The tenor of what relevant literature does exist makes
it clear that there is a need to inform the individual of the
educational opportunities that are available to him: their nature, prerequisites (fees, skills, previous education, and
training), eligibility (age, sex, income, residence, and others), hours, transportation, requirements and facilities, and
rewards (applicability of learned skills, diplomas, certificates,
job placement service, etc.). One report points out that
lack of information about post-secondary vocational schools

is one reason so few blacks attend classes (103). Another
pleads for information about retraining and reeducating programs for poor farmers who are planning to migrate to the
city (217).

There is also little that deals with the adult's information needs related to public schools. What there is simply
affirms the idea that there is such a need. The adult needs
to know what the school is up to, what the children--espe-
cially his child--are studying, and how they are progressing.
The vast majority of parents use their children as a channel
of information about public schools and education; non-parents
use other adults or their children. There is little use of the
mass media (179). This situation is generally deplored, and
it is suggested that there be more vigorous efforts at communicating school-related information. Project Public Information is an example of one attempt to maximize school-
home communications in disadvantaged neighborhoods through
entertaining yet informative formats such as puppet shows,
drama, art and comic books (242).

Recreation

        Although the literature generally acknowledges that all
people have leisure hours to fill with recreation of some
sort, and that this is particularly critical to the aged poor,
there is virtually no substantial treatment of the disadvantaged
adult's information needs related to recreation. There is an
honorable mention in the Voos work (667) and passing references in several others. Nesbitt, et al., have produced the
most complete document on recreation and the disadvantaged
(454). However, even here the discussions of "information
need" are only superficial: formal and informal means of

communicating recreational opportunities need to be exploited; the informal channels are the most important.

Obviously, recreation--and especially information about recreation--is not considered a high priority item by those who study and write about the problems of the disadvantaged.

NOTES

1. It may be this understanding that has stimulated the many "meals on wheels" ventures through which hot, nutritious meals are delivered to the homes of isolated aged people.

2. While some reports (e.g., 49) argue that transportation is much less of a barrier to employment of the poor than we generally imagine, others are contradictory. One study concluded that employment does not increase as transportation barriers are removed. Another report claimed that transportation considerations are particularly critical for the rural poor (475; 428).

3. See (595, p. 219, fn.)

4. The Miami-Dade County study is a rare exploration of the knowledge of the political process among white, black and Spanish groups. Extent and sources of knowledge and attitudes toward county government were major variables. However, the data are so isolated that even tentative generalizations to other localities is extremely risky. Comparable data from other sites is needed to establish the universality of these results.

V

WHO ARE THE INFORMATION POOR?

Below, the literature that pertains to major groups of disadvantaged adults is analyzed briefly. Only the salient points are reported here--the points that distinguish one group from other disadvantaged groups in terms of communication patterns, information seeking behavior or information needs.

Mexican-Americans, Puerto Ricans, and Other Spanish-Speaking

To a great extent, disadvantaged persons are disadvantaged by language. Some groups are simply undereducated: they may be functionally illiterate; their speaking vocabularies may be extraordinarily limited. Other groups have not just been undereducated, they have been educated in a language that is alien in one way or another to the dominant culture. American urban blacks who have grown up with street language are one such group. Certainly immigrants, especially the large groups of Puerto Ricans, Mexican-Americans and other Spanish-speaking, are another.

The literature related to the Spanish-speaking in America points out that language is a constant barrier to communication and information. Even though considerable effort has been spent in recent years trying to overcome the problem, language is still responsible for a considerable gap between the Spanish-Americans and the information that is available to the majority of Americans. The Spanish publications,

78

Spanish radio and television, and Spanish newspaper columns
still have not been sufficient to close the gap completely.

We can assume that all groups of Spanish-speaking
Americans are isolated to some degree from the dominant
society, and thus from information that sustains the dominant
society. Yet a number of characteristics magnify the isolation of the Mexican-Americans. They are proud of their culture, and especially tenacious of their language. They very
much strive for self-sufficiency. They distrust or dislike
Anglo institutions, such as schools, medical clinics, public
housing, etc.

Interesting patterns of media use are evident. First,
the Mexican-American prefers Spanish-language radio to Spanish-language television (compared with the overwhelming pref-
erence for television among other disadvantaged groups).
Second, the poorer, more ethnically isolated, older, and
women prefer Spanish-language media over other-language
media (243).

American Indians and Eskimos

When discussing their information environment, the
American Indian and Eskimo have more in common than not.
Although it is risky to be very specific in characterizing such
a diverse group of people, some general observations can be
made. For the most part, we are talking about non-urban
Indians and Eskimos.

Like other disadvantaged groups, the American Indian
or Eskimo is isolated from the dominant culture and from
the information in it. They are isolated environmentally:
their communities are remote both in terms of distances and
communications links. They are isolated personally: they

distrust or fear the white man and his agencies. They are
isolated culturally: English may be only their second or
third language; shamanism (folk medicine) is still widely
accepted (68;203;479).

Associated with their cultural isolation is the paucity
of communication channels available to them. They tend to
have fewer radios, televisions, newspapers, books, magazines, phones, and community organizations than the general
population (417;450). There is a clear need for improved
channels of information from community to community and
from community to the world at large (479). There is an
acute lack of two-way channels.

In addition, a few writers make a strong case for new
content in the communication, content that speaks to the Indian or Eskimo in terms of his own language and culture,
not in terms of the dominant urban culture. The irrelevance
of content is one of the major criticisms of the Anik project,
a communications satellite that attempts to link scattered
Eskimo communities with the rest of the modern world (479;
344).

There are few information needs unique to the American Indian or Eskimo. For the Indian, the National Indian
Education Association studies provide considerable evidence
that his areas of interest are similar to the general population (448;449;450). Emphases and fine specifics will vary,
of course. And there are a few broad areas of unique information need that stand out: treaty rights and land claims,
confused jurisdictional disputes among tribe, state and nation,
and Indian or Eskimo culture. Also, they frequently share
with other disadvantaged groups the need for considerable information about welfare programs--public assistance, medical care, food stamps, etc.

Poor Black Americans ... and White

The spate of research on the urban blacks has generated a wealth of reports that deal wholly or partially with
them as distinct from other groups in society.   Sixty-nine
documents on the health, employment, education, housing,
consumer or general communications needs or behavior of
the American blacks were found to be related in one degree
or another to their information needs.

Generally speaking, low-income blacks exhibit media-
related behavior similar to low-income whites, only somewhat more so.   That is, both low-income groups differ from
the general population in the way they use and value the mass
media; but blacks differ more markedly than whites (247).

Even more than low-income whites, low-income blacks
use electronic media to the exclusion of reading (246).
They are more likely to own a record player (247).

They tend to use the mass media more heavily for
socialization purposes (231;247).

They are more inclined to use personal channels for
seeking information most of the time (246;46).   However,
in some special situations, they rely more strongly on the
formal channels of search; for example, in job hunting
(347;502).

Low-income whites and blacks show no consistent differences in the media they prefer for local news.   In
descending order, they choose radio, television, newspapers, and people (246).

Overall, disadvantaged black Americans are not strik-
ingly different from other disadvantaged Americans in their
communications and information needs or behavior.

Appalachians

Perhaps more than any other disadvantaged group except the aging American, the Appalachian is resigned to grind-
ing poverty.   Strongly fatalistic, he relinquishes his destiny

to the external forces that impinge on his life. He despairs
quietly, accepting his lot in life and suspicious of the social
programs that are designed for his aid (495). As with other
groups who share this outlook, the Appalachian can be expected to perceive fewer soluble problems in his life and
where he does identify a problem, to see it less often than
average as a lack of information. Thus he will probably
search for information less often and less actively when he
does.

Hayes and Shelby have produced the most important
document related to the information needs of Appalachians.
The report paints a picture of information needs that bear a
striking resemblance to the needs of most other disadvantaged
groups. At the same time the report supports other data
that suggest that the Appalachian is extraordinarily dependent
on interpersonal networks for his information needs (274a).
Since Appalachians are both rural (farm) and urban (small
mining towns), they share communication and information
seeking habits with both rural and urban disadvantaged groups.
One channel of information, though, may be employed much
more by the Appalachian: the extended family. The large
kinship network that is available to every adult provides a
rapid and convincing channel through which information is
transferred within the community. As well, as the younger
members migrate to industrial cities, communication with the
"stem family" back home is frequent enough to bring information into the community from the world at large (81).

Like other non-urban groups with a relatively high
probability of migrating to the city, the Appalachian can be
expected to need information that will help him find a job, a
place to live, perhaps temporary public assistance, training
and educational opportunities, etc. (469;274a).

Poor Farmers

There is evidence that the poor farmer has less of the mass media physically available at home than the high income farmer. But there is also evidence indicating that the poor farmer doesn't differ significantly from the high income farmer in the amount of time spent using the media (59). In general, the patterns of communication that differentiate rich from poor, black from white and educated from uneducated populations in the city operate also in the farm environment (see 605).

The literature (e. g., 169) decries the poor farmer's widespread ignorance of social programs aimed at helping him through instruction, financial aid, or farming assistance. And the necessity of disseminating information through personal contact--friends, suppliers, other farmers, extension workers--is underlined (605;169).

Migrant Workers

Migrant communities "have developed a communications system for passing along information regarding matters that enhance or threaten their economic survival" (600, p. 311). This is one of the most direct statements to be found on information, communications and the migrant worker. There is no elaboration.

There are a number of articles on health and nutrition from which we can deduce an appreciable information need in the areas of preventive health care, food purchasing and food preparation. Another assortment of articles indicates a fairly critical need for improved information on available jobs. Beyond this, the literature is sparse.

The virtual absence of any systematic inquiry into the

flow, utilization, or impact of information in the migrant
camp or the migrant world at large labels this as an area
that is wide open for study.   As well, field experimentation
would yield useful insight into optimal modes of information
delivery in this unique subculture.

Aging Adults

> "Probably one of the most serious problems
> facing elderly people today is the lack of in-
> formation and knowledge about existing pro-
> grams and the available community resources
> which could meet some of their needs" (5,
> p. 34).

There is a great body of writing related to the aging
American and information.   Approximately eighty documents
were examined and judged relevant to the subject.   Taken as
a whole, they provide a fairly consistent picture of the plight
of the aging adult.

While most disadvantaged persons are born into their
particular disadvantages--blackness, poverty, language barriers, etc.--that is not necessarily the case for the aging
adult.   Great numbers of Americans grow into the disadvan-
tagements of old age.   Even the seemingly secure middle-
class, middle-aged adult of today may be the disadvantaged
senior citizen of tomorrow, as his income falls and costs
rise, health deteriorates, mental faculties fail, and mate and
friends die or become institutionalized.   No one is immune
to the social and physical poverty of old age.

The aging adult is isolated in his environment even
more than any other disadvantaged group.   With the exception
of a few ethnic groups in America--Mexican-Americans, for
instance (106)--the aging man or woman is gradually locked
out of the very sub-culture that he was once part of.   Through

deaths, infirmity, migrations of friends and relatives, and retirement he is gradually disengaged from the corps of personal resources that he once enjoyed. As he watches his own social disengagement, he witnesses, too, the deterioration of his body and a greatly impaired financial power. He grows lonely and fearful. He despairs. He begins to avoid social contact; his touch with the outside world diminishes (123).

It is often held that the use of the mass media decreases with age (291). Still, there is a slight amount of evidence that as the aging adult is disengaged from his social world he substitutes by relying more heavily on the mass media (110). There is more consistent evidence about how he relies on the various media: newspapers become increasingly important as a source of information (309).

A number of the disadvantages of old age relate to information. First, social disengagement dramatically expands the aging adult's leisure time and at the same time reduces the number of people with whom he might pass that time. In terms of information, it could be formulated that the most obvious need is for information on appropriate recreational opportunities, and on programs designed to heighten social activities.

Second, impaired mobility, hearing, sight, and mental processes may interfere with information-receiving capacities, making it more difficult to gain access to or process information. New patterns of information-seeking may be required: telephones instead of live on-site communication; audio recordings or large-print books instead of ordinary reading material; sound-boosters on televisions and radios.

As well, failing health brings with it an extra expense to maintain health--expense in terms of worry and money. Yet the aging adult's universal concern for his health does not

appear to make him more knowledgeable about health matters.
There is evidence that those over 65 possess less health-
related knowledge than those under 65, even when controlling
for education (210). There is a widespread need for information on nutrition, drugs, patent medicines, and sources of
inexpensive health care. Preventive information and counseling is needed in areas that are prone to quackery--nostrums,
fraudulent medical practice, hearing aids, and others.

Again as the result of failing health, there is a per-
sistent need for information on nursing care, nursing and retirement homes and homemaking assistance (hot meal services, housekeepers, etc.).

Third: money. Income falls, costs rise and what
was once an adequate standard of living may fall below the
poverty level. More than any other area, housing appears
to be the most critical complaint of the aging adult. Spiral-
ling taxes and reduced financial resources conspire to lock
him into cheap and substandard housing often located in de-
pressed, unsafe neighborhoods. He needs information on inexpensive, standard housing and on programs that help defray
rising real estate taxes.

Fourth: Due to depleted financial resources, the aging
American is forced to rely more and more on public programs for life support--social security, Medicare, free transportation, etc. To a lone individual though, these programs
appear to be numerous, varied and sometimes contradictory.
Finding his way through them in order to receive all of his
just entitlements is a bewildering and endless process. There
is a critical need for information services that will dispense
information on the various social agencies and their programs
in an aggressive manner, not waiting till the client approaches,
but trying to anticipate his needs and making contact with him

first. To some extent the nature of the problem has been recognized by society. It is evidenced not only by the amount of writing on the subject, but also by the numerous accounts of information and referral activities designed for aging populations. (See 649 for a list of I and R services for the aging.)

Prisoners

The world of the prisoner to a large extent looks like the outside world in microcosm. The social processes are similar. The demographic characteristics, intelligence, skills, and others, resemble the general population more than they resemble other disadvantaged groups.

The prisoner's disadvantage lies in his lack of access to the outside world. His communications system, and therefore his information exchange, is inhibited by the censorship imposed by the prison authorities. It works in two dimensions: within the institution, and between the institution and the outside world.

As evidenced by the literature, the prisoner's primary concern in the area of information is to gain free exchange with individuals and open access to published materials outside the institution. His interest lies predominantly in the area of legal information. He is in need of nothing short of a complete law library, so that he can apply existing statutes and precedents to his own case as well as to his civil problems (divorce, mortgage, etc.) (317). He is likewise in need of a legal alerting service that will inform him of new statutes and rulings that have potential bearing on his conviction, of shifts in his trial dates, success of conviction appeals, and parole criteria.

The literature provides evidence that there has been

considerable change in recent years.   Prison authorities appear to be more willing than before to allow prisoners free access to legal information and open sharing of that information among themselves.   Ombudsman services have been established in some institutions (628).   The Supreme Court decisions of Younger v. Gilmore and Johnson v. Avery, asserting the right of prisoners to have a law library available to them and to engage in legal activity on behalf of others, have undoubtedly added impetus to the changes (501; 689).

Beyond that, the prisoner's information needs are no longer unique, although they are of course colored by his unique environment.   Even within the limited range of the institution, he needs consumer information (commissary prices), health information (examination schedules), education information (course schedules and training opportunities), employment information (prison jobs available), crisis information, etc.   And to the extent that he maintains interests in the outside world, his information needs resemble every other citizen's.

The Blind or Deaf

The literature on the information needs of the blind or deaf person is minute.

Unlike other disadvantages, blindness or deafness consists wholly of impairment of a communication channel. Special needs--information needs, for instance--hinge on that impairment.

There are two areas in which there is a need for unique content.   First, the blind and deaf need information about devices that compensate for their disability--where to get them and how to finance them.   Second, they need information on the public and private services that are available specially for them. Other than these, the information needs of the blind and deaf, per se, are similar to the information needs of the general population; the sparse literature supports this assertion.

The major information-related need of the blind or deaf is for new channels of communication. Information must be delivered in new packages if he is to partake of it. He has to have new ways of communicating in order to compensate for his lack of vision or hearing. Extensive captioning on television for the deaf and special maps that help the blind travel to new places by themselves are two inventions designed for the channel needs of the blind and deaf (66;1).

VI

DIRECTIONS FOR THE FUTURE

The literature reveals a fair number of studies that have focused directly on the information environment of the disadvantaged. There is still another corpus of research from which inferences can be drawn. Yet, viewed as a whole, it presents a picture of unintegrated research efforts from which we can generalize only tentatively. In addition, there have been many efforts at testing methods of packaging and delivering information on various topics for various groups. These efforts, too, have been small and isolated. Their results are situation-specific and permit virtually no usable comparisons from group to group, topic to topic, or site to site.

In the future, coordinating scattered research and demonstration and undertaking broad-based, long term research and demonstration will add greatly to what we know about the disadvantaged American's universe of information. The need for coordinating future research efforts is underscored by Robert Bundy's proposal for a National Research/ Action Center for the Long Range Study of Human Information Needs. He suggests that such a center is needed

> (1) to expose the range of current human information problems among diverse groups in the population, (2) to consolidate and extend the work of current research efforts dealing with particular facets of human information problems, (3) to identify promising approaches for serving human information

needs by means of existing technological capabilities
and existing information systems, and (4) to develop integrated forecasts for describing emerging human information problems in the wake of already
recognized social and technological trends. All of
this suggests many different institutional approaches
for studying and dealing with human information
problems. Needed immediately, however, is the
establishment of a national center of research activity institutionalized around the specific study of
human information problems and supported by strong
linkages with other national/international research
and planning centers. This approach would provide
a continuing research forum and bring to the public
attention the seriousness of providing for human information needs and assessing the long range characteristics of human information needs [89, p. 4].

Stating specific hypotheses may be premature at this
point. The number of researchable hypotheses is almost
countless. It will serve us better to point out broader areas
in which further inquiry would help us understand and respond
to the information needs of disadvantaged Americans.

In any inquiry it will be valuable to compare the disadvantaged group under investigation with the general adult
population, in order to maintain perspective. Too often the
disadvantaged groups are dealt with in isolation, or they are
not analyzed separately in studies of general populations.
Thus, relative differences and similarities go unnoted.

While there have been numerous demonstrations and
"experiments" aimed at dispensing information to disadvantaged adults, the efforts have been buried in a specific situation. There has been little attempt to produce generalizable knowledge. Consequently the myriad reports of new
services, new techniques and new staffing patterns provide
little, if any, understanding that can be transferred to other
situations. There is a vacuum in the field that can be filled
by conducting carefully controlled experimental research

related to the packaging and delivery of information to disadvantaged groups.   Major variables in such research include: channels of information, funding and staffing of the information facility, content of messages, frequency and format of delivery, style of delivery, predispositions of the individual, his personal characteristics, and the setting in which information is received.   Special emphasis should be laid on a comparison of information packaging and delivery systems along two gross dimensions: topic and target group.

The two most popular suggestions for remedying information problems of the disadvantaged are: more communication through television and more communication through interpersonal contact.   Special attention should be paid to the effectiveness of various configurations of these two important channels.   The RFD program in Wisconsin, while it provides fairly complete documentation of some interesting efforts, is difficult to generalize from, since the experimental variables are largely uncontrolled (528).   In Operation Gap-Stop, an experiment in communicating with the poor, the variables were controlled, but the methodology somewhat limits the findings (420).   Nonetheless, the study does begin to explore the impact of information on behavior.

Below are a number of areas for future inquiry.   The questions presented here will yield most often to survey and field experimental research.

How do various channels of information, formal and informal, mix in the broad range of an individual's everyday problems?   Which channels are received, accepted, sought, or acted upon for which purposes, and by what kind of person?   It is important to point out again that rather than small fragmented studies, a larger integrated research effort is needed.   White has tested a method to establish the value

of various channels of information to the individual. It con-
sisted of a funnelling technique in which the respondent is
asked to compare pairs of channels as to their value in communicating new farming practices. The "most valuable"
channel from each pair is then compared with the "most valuable" channel from another pair. The process continues
until the respondent finally judges one channel the most valuable (694).

How is information diffused within a given type of disadvantaged community? What combination of communication
channels is most effective in disseminating information to,
say, the diffuse and transient migrant populations? This
would entail studying:

1. the flow of information through the formal and in-
    formal channels: mass media, social agencies,
    friends, relatives, community opinion leaders, etc.;
2. the generation and revision of information within the
    community and the importation of information from
    outside; and
3. the interaction among formal and informal channels,
    in order to understand
    a. the way in which they interact
    b. the resulting information level within the
        community
    c. the speed of diffusion of information.

The absence of any substantial investigation of the information universe of the migrant worker makes this target group
especially ripe for study. Wolpert's study of information dif-
fusion among Swedish farmers might serve as a model for
future investigations (714).

Parker speculates that, for the general adult population, interpersonal communication is relied upon for cueing,
while print is relied upon for specific information--as is the
case in the scientific community (484). Does this hold for
disadvantaged Americans?

There is relatively little empirical data on the levels
of public information among the disadvantaged populations
(and even among the general population), particularly in the
area of the political process, community affairs and government (see 595, p. 219 fn.).

In one report, Mendelsohn explores a simple model
that he calls "information distance"--the proportion of respondents who are informed on a given specific topic, minus the
proportion of respondents who are uninformed on the same
topic (420). Further testing of this model may provide a
convenient way of describing the information "mass" that
exists within disadvantaged populations.

A number of unanswered questions exist in the area
of motivation and predisposition. At this point we understand
very little about the complex interaction of the factors that
predispose an individual to seek or accept or apply information: social norms, personal values and attitudes, the specific situation, intensity of perceived need, the individual's
information-seeking history and other external and internal
elements. (Warner suggests that his data "may indicate that
the active information-seekers have more influential acquaint-
ances who are willing to assist them than do the less active
information-seekers" [677, p. 6:31].) While several studies
approach the question, they commonly employ only a limited
number of variables--say, sense of helplessness, anomie,
degree of fatalism, and level of education--within a very
limited situation. Questions about motivation are particularly
difficult to answer. It may be that the present state of mo-
tivational research will not permit great advances in our
knowledge at this time.

Parker asserts that the perceived need for information
is lower among lesser educated people (484). The Warner

report supports him with substantial data (677). Parker goes on, though, to speculate that when a <u>perceived</u> need is lacking, affiliation-need, the simple drive to do things with other people, is not of itself sufficient to stimulate interpersonal information-seeking. Currently there is no evidence that tests this hypothesis.

Are information facilities dedicated to specific topics and/or specific disadvantaged groups more effective in reaching the disadvantaged populations than facilities that dispense information on a variety of topics, or to the general population?

Is information disseminated more effectively through many separate private and social agencies, or through a single autonomous information facility? What kinds of information are best dispensed through general information facilities? Through private agencies? Through specialized social agencies?

How is information used in problem-solving? What is the relationship between information received or sought and subsequent decisions and activity? There has been very little experimental study of the actual impact of information on behavior. We do have studies that explore, ex post facto, associations between <u>remembered</u> information-related behavior and <u>remembered</u> subsequent activity. But we have seldom explored, through experimental research, the extent to which new increments of information affect the life of the individual, or vice versa. (One interesting report (598), for example, suggests that increased knowledge may be an <u>effect</u> of social mobility, not a cause.) The areas of drug abuse and alcoholism are particularly lacking in research of this kind. In this broad area we would be especially interested in:

Changes in the quality of life--for the individual or

community, in both the long and short term
Changes in service demands on local and non-local
agencies
Changes in the individual's decision-making process and
habits
Changes in the actual decisions made.

In his study of "urban knowledge" of rural Venezuelan families who migrated to Ciudad Guayana, McGinn provides a
sophisticated example of an attempt to identify behavioral
changes that result from information (400).

VIII

BIBLIOGRAPHY

These documents relate in some degree to the information needs, communications patterns, and information seeking behavior of the disadvantaged American. The starred numbers indicate the ones with the most substantial content along these lines. The entries are arranged alphabetically. For more specific access to most items in the bibliography, turn to the Topical Index.

* 1 Abt Associates, Inc. Transportation Needs of the Handi-
      capped: Travel Barriers. Cambridge, Mass. 1969.
      (NTIS PB 187 327)

  2 Administration and Effectiveness of the EO Loan Pro-
      gram for Low-Income Rural Families under the
      Farmers Home Administration, Department of Agri-
      culture. Report to the Congress by the Comptroller
      General of the United States. Washington, D.C.:
      Government Printing Office, 1969.

  3 Adult Referral and Information Service in Education
      (ARISE). Final Report. Providence, R.I.: Provi-
      dence Public Schools, 1970. (ERIC ED 061 479)

  4 Afek, Luella B. "A Health Referral System for Migrants,"
      Health Services Reports 88:31-33, January 1973.

  5 Aging in St. Louis: A Study of the Aging Information and
      Direction Service. St. Louis: Health and Welfare
      Council of Metropolitan St. Louis, 1970.

  6 Alexander, Benjamin H. "Chronic Illness--Fact of Life
      for the Rural Poor," Hospitals 43:71-74, July 1,
      1969.

  7 Alexander, William M. "Large Group Decision-Making
      Assisted by a Feedback System; A Preliminary Study,"

Rocky Mountain Social Science Journal 6:1-8, October 1969.

8   Allen, Thomas H. "Mass Media Use Patterns in a Negro Ghetto," Journalism Quarterly 45:525-527, Autumn 1968.

9   Alper, S. W., and T. R. Leidy. "Impact of Information Transmission through Television," Public Opinion Quarterly 33:556-562, Winter 1969-70.

10 Ambrosino, Robert J., and Anne M. Anzola. "Keeping Healthy After Sixty by Two-Way Radio," Health Services Reports 87:583-587, August/September 1972.

11 Amemiya, Eiji C. "Practices that Negatively Affect the Self-Image of the Inmate," American Journal of Correction 30:25-26, May/June 1968.

12 American Rehabilitation Foundation. Institute for Interdisciplinary Studies. Information and Referral Services: Follow-up, Working Draft. Minneapolis: 1971. (ERIC ED 055 637)

13 _____. Information and Referral Services: Interviewing and Information Giving, Working Draft. Minneapolis: 1971. (ERIC ED 055 635)

14 _____. Information and Referral Services: Notes for Managers, Working Draft. Minneapolis: 1971. (ERIC ED 055 633)

15 _____. Information and Referral Services: Reaching Out, Working Draft. Minneapolis: 1971. (ERIC ED 055 640)

16 _____. Information and Referral Services: Referral Procedures, Working Draft. Minneapolis: 1971. (ERIC ED 055 636)

*17 _____. Information and Referral Services: The Resource File, Working Draft. Minneapolis: 1971. (ERIC ED 055 634)

*18 _____. Information and Referral Services: The Role of Advocacy, Working Draft. Minneapolis: 1971. (ERIC ED 055 639)

19 Anderson, Darrell, and John A. Niemi. Adult Education
   and the Disadvantaged Adult. Syracuse: Syracuse
   University and ERIC Clearinghouse on Adult Education, 1970. (Occasional Paper No. 22)

20 Archibald, Kathleen, and Ben Bagdikian. Televised Ombudsman. New York: The Rand Corporation, 1968.
   (NTIS AD 669 319)

21 Atkinson, Maxwell. "The Samaritans and the Elderly:
   Some Problems in Communication Between a Suicide
   Prevention Scheme and a Group with a High Suicide
   Rate," Social Science and Medicine 5:483-490, Octo-
   ber 1971.

22 Atlanta University. School of Library Services; Emory
   University. Division of Librarianship. Public Library Service to the Disadvantaged, Proceedings of
   an Institute, Atlanta, December 7-8, 1967. Atlanta:
   Emory University Bookstore, 1969.

23 Atwood, H. Mason, and Joe Ellis. "The Concept of
   Need: An Analysis for Adult Education," Adult
   Leadership 19:210-212, 244, January 1971.

24 Baird, Russell N. The Penal Press. Evanston, Ill.:
   Northwestern University Press, 1967.

25 Barr, Sherman. "The Social Agency as a Disseminator
   of Information." In Individual and Group Services
   in the Mobilization for Youth Experience, edited by
   Harold H. Weissman. New York: Association Press,
   1969, pp. 54-61.

26 Barton, Ann, and Virginia Gilchrist. "Needs and Interests of Young Homemakers Living in Two Low-Income Housing Projects," Journal of Home Economics
   62:389-392, June 1970.

27 Barvick, William M. "Legal Services and the Rural
   Poor," University of Kansas Law Review 15:537-551,
   May 1967.

28 Bass, Floyd L. "Impact of the Black Experience on Attitudes Toward Higher Education," Adult Education
   22:207-217, Spring 1972.

29 Batchelder, Alan. "Poverty; The Special Case of the
    Negro," American Economic Review 55:530-540, May
    1965.

30 Baum, Daniel J., and J. W. Mohr. "Toward a Free
    Housing Market," Rutgers Law Review 24:712-751,
    Summer 1970.

31 Beasley, Joseph D., Carl L. Harter, and Ann Fischer.
    "Attitudes and Knowledge Relevant to Family Planning
    Among New Orleans Negro Women," American Jour-
    nal of Public Health 56:1847-1857, November 1966.

32 _____, and Ralph F. Frankowski. "Utilization of a
    Family Planning Program by the Poor Population of
    a Metropolitan Area," Milbank Memorial Fund Quar-
    terly 48:241-282, April 1970.

33 Beck, Mildred B., Sidney H. Newman, and Sarah Lewitt.
    "Abortion: A National Public and Mental Health Prob-
    lem--Past, Present, and Proposed Research," Amer-
    ican Journal of Public Health 59:2131-2143, Decem-
    ber 1969.

*34 Beiler, Ross C. A Survey of Communications Concern-
    ing Local Government that Reach or Are Circulated
    by Members of the Three Primary Ethnic Aggregates
    Resident in Dade County, Florida: Some Tabulations
    and Highlights. Coral Gables: University of Miami,
    Center for Urban Studies, 1969. (NTIS PB 191 211)

35 Bellin, Seymour S., and H. Jack Geiger. "Actual Public
    Acceptance of Neighborhood Health Centers by the
    Urban Poor," Journal of the American Medical Asso-
    ciation 214:2147-2153, December 21, 1970.

36 Bennette, Guy. "San Francisco: Down These Meaningful
    Streets: The Fillmore Street Reference Project,"
    Wilson Library Bulletin 43:872-875, May 1969.

37 Bergman, Moe. "Changes in Hearing with Age," Geron-
    tologist 11:148-151, Summer 1971.

38 Bergner, Lawrence, and Alonzo S. Yerby. "Low Income
    and Barriers to Use of Health Services," The New
    England Journal of Medicine 278:541-546, March 7,
    1968.

39   Bernard, Viola W. "Why People Become the Victims of
      Medical Quackery, "American Journal of Public Health
      55:1142-1147, August 1965.

*40   Berry, Leonard L. "The Low-Income Marketing System;
      An Overview, " Journal of Retailing 48:44-63, 90,
      Summer 1972.

41   _____, and Paul J. Solomon. "Generalizing About
      Low-Income Food Shoppers: A Word of Caution, "
      Journal of Retailing 47:41-51+, Summer 1971.

42   Blake, Robert R., and others. Beliefs and Attitudes
      about Contraception among the Poor. Chapel Hill:
      University of North Carolina, Carolina Population
      Center, 1969. (Monograph 5)

43   Blank, Marie Latz. "Recent Research Findings on Prac-
      tice with the Aging, " Social Casework 52:382-408,
      June 1971.

44   Blau, Zena S. "Exposure to Child-Rearing Experts: A
      Structural Interpretation of Class-Color Differences, "
      American Journal of Sociology 69:596-608, May 1964.

45   Bliss, Peggy. "Legal Services on the Spot, " American
      Bar Association Journal 53:724-725, August 1967.

*46   Block, Carl E. "Communicating with the Poor." In
      Libraries and Neighborhood Information Centers,
      papers presented at the 17th Allerton Park Institute,
      October 24-27, 1971, edited by Carol L. Kronus
      and Linda Crowe. Urbana: University of Illinois,
      Graduate School of Library Science, 1972, pp. 30-
      49.

*47   _____. "Communicating with the Urban Poor: An
      Exploratory Inquiry, " Journalism Quarterly 47:3-11,
      Spring 1970.

48   _____. "Prepurchase Search Behavior of Low-Income
      Households, " Journal of Retailing 48:3-15, Spring
      1972.

*49   _____ and others. The Badge of Poverty, the St.
      Louis Report. Columbia: University of Missouri,
      Regional Rehabilitation Research Institute, 1970.
      (Research Series #4)

50 Bloom, Martin. "Measurement of Socioeconomic Status
    of the Aged: New Thoughts on an Old Subject,"
    Gerontologist 12:375-378, Winter 1972.

51 _____, and M. Nielson. "Older Person in Need of
    Protective Services," Social Casework 52:500-509,
    October 1971.

52 Blum, Edward H. "Municipal Services." In Planning
    Community Information Utilities, edited by Harold
    Sackman and B. Boehm. Montvale, N.J.: AFIPS
    Press, 1972, pp. 45-68.

53 Bogue, Donald J. "Acceptance of a Family Planning
    Program by the Rural Poor, Summary of an Experi-
    ment in Alabama." In Rural Poverty in the United
    States, by President's National Advisory Commission
    on Rural Poverty. Washington, D.C.: Government
    Printing Office, 1968, pp. 389-412.

54 _____. "Family Planning in the Negro Ghettos of
    Chicago," Milbank Memorial Fund Quarterly 48:283-
    307, April 1970.

55 Bonser, Charles F., and Jack R. Wentworth. A Study
    of Adult Information Needs in Indiana. Bloomington:
    Indiana State Library, 1970. (Indiana Library Studies,
    Report No. 3)

56 Booth, Alan, and Nicholas Babchuk. "Informal Medical
    Opinion Leadership among the Middle Aged and El-
    derly," Public Opinion Quarterly 36:87-94, Spring
    1972.

57 _____, and Alan B. Knox. "Participation in Adult
    Education Agencies and Personal Influence," Sociol-
    ogy of Education 40:275-277, Summer 1967.

58 Borstelmann, L. J. "Missionaries or Educators? Par-
    ent Education for Poverty Families," Community
    Mental Health Journal 5:149-155, 1969.

*59 Bostian, Lloyd R. "Socio-Economic Factors Associated
    with Communications Behavior of Farm Operators in
    Selected Wisconsin Communities." (Unpublished Ph.D.
    dissertation, University of Wisconsin, 1959.)

60 Bourne, Charles P., and others. Preliminary Investiga-
    tion of Present and Potential Library and Information
    Service Needs: Final Report. Berkeley: University
    of California, Institute of Library Research, Febru-
    ary 1973.

61 Bowe, Frank G. "Non-White Deaf Persons: Educational,
    Psychological and Occupational Considerations: A
    Review of the Literature, " American Annals of the
    Deaf 116:357-361, June 1971.

62 _____. "Role of the Paraprofessional in Inner-City
    Services to Deaf Persons, " Journal of Rehabilitation
    of the Deaf 6:120-122, October 1972.

63 Bowen, Robert O. "Effect of Informal Dissemination of
    Health Information, " Journal of School Health 42:342-
    344, June 1972.

64 Bowles, John E. "Information Control Behaviors and the
    Political Effectiveness of Low-Income Urban Blacks. "
    (Unpublished Ph. D. dissertation, Michigan State Uni-
    versity, 1971.)

65 Bowling, George St. Clair. "The Effects of Instructional
    Programs on Knowledge about Medicare and Attitudes
    Towards Proposed Social Programs. " (Unpublished
    Ph. D. dissertation, Boston University, School of Edu-
    cation, 1970.)

*66 Boyd, Francis W. "Needs of the Deaf: Remarks by
    Francis W. Boyd, " Hearing and Speech News 37:7+
    28, September/October 1969.

67 Boyd, J., and E. A. Vader. "Captioned Television for
    the Deaf, " American Annals of the Deaf 117:34-37,
    February 1972.

68 Bozof, Richard P. "Some Navaho Attitudes Toward Avail-
    able Medical Care, " American Journal of Public
    Health 62:1620-1624, December 1972.

*69 Bradshaw, Thomas F. "Jobseeking Methods Used by Un-
    employed Workers, " Monthly Labor Review 96:35-40,
    February 1973.

*70 Brand, Horst. Poverty Area Profiles, the Job Search of

Ghetto Workers, Bedford-Stuyvesant, Central Harlem, East Harlem, South Bronx. Washington, D.C.: Department of Labor, Labor Statistics Bureau, Regional Reports (Mid-Atlantic Regional Office), 1971.

*71 Brand, Jean. "Family Planning Information: Do Low-Income Families Need and Want It?" Journal of Home Economics 64:2-5, May 1972.

72 Briar, Scott. "Welfare from Below: Recipients' Views of the Public Welfare System," California Law Review 54:370-385, 1966.

73 Brightman, I., and others. "Knowledge and Utilization of Health Resources by Public Assistance Recipients," American Journal of Public Health 48:188-199, February 1958, and 48:319-327, March 1958.

74 Brochin, Bridget. An Acculturation Problem Check List Study of the Band of Chippewa Indians of the Turtle Mountain Reservation, Belcourt, North Dakota. Indiana, Pa.: Indiana University of Pennsylvania, 1969.

75 Brody, Barbara L. "New Approaches to Patient Recruitment and a View of Hospital Programs." Paper presented at the annual meeting of the American Association of Planned Parenthood Physicians, Atlanta, Ga., April 3, 1967.

76 Brody, Elaine J., and Stanley J. Brody. "A Ninety-Minute Inquiry: The Expressed Needs of the Elderly," Gerontologist 10:99-106, Summer 1970.

77 Brooks, Jean S. "Approach to an Information and Resource Service for Older Adults," AHIL Quarterly 12:14-15, Spring/Summer 1972.

78 Brown, Carol. "Putting the Law in Order," Synergy issue no. 36:8-9, Spring 1972.

*79 Brown, Eleanor F. Library Service to the Disadvantaged. Metuchen, N.J.: Scarecrow Press, 1971.

80 Brown, Emory J., and others. Evaluation of a Goods and Nutrition Educational Program for Low-Income Families in Wilkes-Barre, Pa. University Park, Pa.: Pennsylvania State University, Cooperative Extension Service, 1965. (Extension Studies 32)

81 Brown, James S., and Harry K. Schwarzweller. "The
    Appalachian Family." In Change in Rural Appalachia;
    Implications for Action Programs, edited by John D.
    Photiadas and Harry K. Schwarzweller. Philadelphia:
    University of Pennsylvania Press, 1970, pp. 85-97.

82 Brown, Thomas E. "Sex Education and Life in the Black
    Ghetto," Religious Education 64:450-458, November-
    December 1969.

83 Brown, William H., Jr. "Access to Housing: The Role
    of the Real Estate Industry," Economic Geography
    48:66-78, January 1972.

84 Brudney, Juliet F. The Janus Project: Advocacy and
    Service for the Elderly Relocatee. Philadelphia:
    University of Pennsylvania, Institute for Environ-
    mental Studies, 1969.

85 Bruner, Richard W. "Why the Poor Stay Poor," Think
    32:18-22, May/June 1966.

86 Bullock, Paul. "Employment Problems of the Mexican
    American," Industrial Relations 3:37-50, May 1964.

87 _____. "Youth in the Labor Market: Employment
    Patterns and Career Goals in Watts and East Los
    Angeles," Poverty and Human Resources Abstracts
    7:163-178, June 1972.

*88 Bundy, Mary Lee. "Urban Information and Public Li-
    braries: A Design for Service," Library Journal 97:
    161-169, January 15, 1972.

*89 Bundy, Robert. "A Discussion Document Exploring the
    Need for a Center for the Long Range Study of Hu-
    man Information Needs." In Urban Information Spe-
    cialist Project: An Educational Program to Prepare
    Community Information Workers in the Urban Setting.
    A Request for Renewal. Prepared by the Urban In-
    formation Specialist Project Planning Committee.
    (n. p.) 1971.

90 Buswell, Christa H. "Reading and the Aged," Wilson
    Library Bulletin 45:467-476, January 1971.

91 Butler, Robert N. "Why Are Older Consumers So Sus-
    ceptible?" Geriatrics 23:83-88, December 1968.

92 "Buying Tips for the Blind--By Telephone," The Evening
    Bulletin (Philadelphia), April 6, 1972.

93 Cady, Thomas C. "Special Needs of Appalachia," Ten-
    nessee Law Review 37:3-16, Fall 1969.

94 Caliguri, Joseph P. "Speakers Bureau on Drug Informa-
    tion: One Experience," Journal of School Health 42:
    333-334, June 1972.

*95 Campbell, Rex R., and Susan A. Mulvey. Perception of
    Job Opportunities among Low Income Groups in Mis-
    souri. Columbia: University of Missouri, Agricul-
    ture Experiment Station, 1967. (NTIS PB 177 868)

96 Canadian Welfare Council. Division on Aging. Informa-
    tion and Referral Services for the Aged in Canada.
    Ottawa: Canadian Council on Social Development,
    1970.

97 Cannell, Charles F., and Harvey Sharp. "Impact of
    1955-56 Detroit Newspaper Strike," Journalism Quar-
    terly 35:26-35, Winter 1958.

98 Cantilli, Edmund J., and June L. Shmelzer, eds. Trans-
    portation and Aging: Selected Issues. Based on Pro-
    ceedings of the Interdisciplinary Workshop on Trans-
    portation and Aging, Washington, D. C., May 24-26,
    1970. Washington, D. C.: Government Printing Of-
    fice, 1970.

99 Cantor, Norman L. "Law and Poor People's Access to
    Health Care," Law and Contemporary Problems 35:
    901-922, Autumn 1970.

100 Caplovitz, David. The Poor Pay More. New York:
    Free Press, 1963.

101 Capriotti, Anthony. Pharmacy and the Poor. Washing-
    ton, D. C.: American Pharmaceutical Association,
    1971. (NTIS PB 210 599)

102 Carbine, Michael E. "Communicating with the Disadvan-
    taged," Manpower 1:2-6, October 1969.

103 Career Education. Papers presented at the 1972 Annual

Meeting of the American Educational Research Association, Chicago, April 15, 1972. Washington, D.C.: American Educational Research Association, 1972. (ERIC ED 062 540)

104 Carlin, Jerome E., and Jan Howard. "Legal Representation and Class Justice," UCLA Law Review 12: 381-437, January 1965.

105 Carp, Frances M. "Communicating with Elderly Mexican-Americans," Gerontologist 10:126-134, Summer 1970.

106 _____. "Housing and Minority Group Elderly," Gerontologist 9:20-24, Spring 1969.

107 Carper, Ellie M. "Media Utilization and the Multi-Handicapped Deaf," Journal of Rehabilitation of the Deaf 6:56-58, October 1972.

108 Cartwright, Walter J., W. G. Steglich, and Ben M. Crouch. "Use of Community Resources among Aged Mexican-Americans," Southwestern Sociological Association Proceedings 19:184-188, April 1969.

109 Casey, Genevieve M. "Public Library Service to the Aging," American Libraries 2:999-1004, October 1971.

110 Cassata, Mary B. "A Study of the Mass Communications Behavior and Social Disengagement Behavior of 177 Members of the Age Center of New England." (Unpublished Ph.D. dissertation, Indiana University, 1967.)

111 Cavanagh, Catherine, and Dorothy Z. Price. "Teaching Decision-Making to the Disadvantaged," Journal of Home Economics 60:337-342, May 1968.

112 Chamber of Commerce of the U.S. Task Force on Economic Growth and Opportunity. The Disadvantaged Poor: Education and Employment. Washington, D.C.: 1966.

113 Chase, Jonathan B. "Migrant Farm Worker in Colorado --the Life and the Law," University of Colorado Law Review 40:45-78, Fall 1967.

114   Chesler, L. G., and H. S. Dordick. Communication
      Goals for Los Angeles, a Working Paper for the Los
      Angeles Goals Program. Santa Monica, Cal.: The
      Rand Corporation, 1968. (P-3769-1)

115   Chesterman, Helen. "The Public Health Nurse and
      Family Planning, " Nursing Outlook 12:32-34, Septem-
      ber 1964.

116   "Chicago Adwomen's Mobile Unit to Aid Ethnic Consum-
      ers, " Advertising Age 39:162, May 20, 1968.

117   Chilman, Catherine S., and Ivor Kraft. "Helping Low-
      Income Parents Through Parent Education Groups, "
      Children 10:127-132, July/August 1963.

*118 Chinn, Austin B. and Edith G. Robins. "Health Aspects
      of Aging. " In The Daily Needs and Interests of Old-
      er People, edited by Adeline M. Hoffman. Spring-
      field, Ill.: Charles C. Thomas, 1970, pp. 209-231.

119   Chladek, Marian. "Nursing Service for Migrant Work-
      ers, " American Journal of Nursing 65:62-65, June
      1965.

120   Christensen, Barlow F. "Lawyer Referral Service: An
      Alternative to Lay-Group Legal Services?" UCLA
      Law Review 12:341-350, January 1965.

121   Citizens Planning Council of Rochester and Monroe Co.,
      Inc. Needs of the Elderly in the Model Cities Area,
      Rochester, N. Y. Rochester: 1970.

122   Clark, Kenneth B. Dark Ghetto, Dilemmas of Social
      Power. New York: Harper, 1967.

*123 Clark, Margaret. "Patterns of Aging Among the Elderly
      Poor of the Inner City, " Gerontologist 11:58-66,
      Spring 1971.

124   Clawson, Marion. "Rural Poverty in the U. S., " Journal
      of Farm Economics 49:1227-1233, December 1967.

125   Clift, Virgil. A Study of Library Services for the Dis-
      advantaged in Buffalo, Rochester and Syracuse. New
      York: New York University, Center for Field Re-
      search and School Services, 1969.

126 Cohen, Nathan, ed. Los Angeles Riots; A Socio-Psy-
     chological Study. Los Angeles: University of Cali-
     fornia, Institute of Government and Public Affairs,
     1967.

127 Cole, George F., and Howard L. Greenberger. "The
     Family Law Concept and the Legal Needs of Welfare
     Recipients," Public Welfare 31:58-62, Winter 1973.

128 Columbia Broadcasting System. White and Negro Atti-
     tudes Towards Race Related Issues and Activities.
     Princeton, N.J.: Public Opinion Research Corpora-
     tion, 1968.

129 "Comics Make the Job Scene," Training in Business and
     Industry 7:27-30, June 1970.

130 Committee on Housing Research and Development. Ac-
     tivities and Attitudes of Public Housing Residents:
     Rockford, Illinois. Champaign: University of Illi-
     nois at Urbana-Champaign, 1971.

131 Community Health Representative, a Changing Philosophy
     of Indian Involvement. Washington, D.C.: Department
     of Health, Education, and Welfare, Public Health Ser-
     vice, Indian Health Survey (n.d.).

132 Conaway, Sister Mary Christine. "Reaching the Un-
     reached 'No Place' People: Migrant Farm Workers,"
     Catholic Library Weekly 43:187-192, December 1971.

133 Consumer Action and War on Poverty, proceedings of a
     conference sponsored by OEO-CAP and The Presi-
     dent's Committee on Consumer Interests, August 12-
     13, 1965, Washington, D.C. (n.p.) 1966.

134 "Consumer Protection Eludes Poor," Media & Consumer
     1:3, March 1973.

135 Consumers' Association of Canada. A Community In-
     formation Network. Ottawa: 1971. (ERIC ED 054
     834)

*136 "The Contact Centre," Library Journal 97:3955-3959,
     December 15, 1972.

137 Corkey, Elizabeth C. "A Family Planning Program for

the Low-Income Family," Journal of Marriage and the Family 26:478-480, November 1964.

138 Cornely, Paul B., and Stanley K. Bigman. "Acquaintance with Municipal Government Health Services in a Low-Income Urban Population," American Journal of Public Health 52:1877-1886, November 1962.

139 _____, and _____. "Extent of Selected Immunizations among a Low-Income Urban Population," Journal of the National Medical Association 55:213-217, May 1963.

*140 _____, and _____. "Some Considerations in Changing Health Attitudes," Children 10:23-28, January/February 1963.

141 _____, _____, and Dorothy D. Watts. "Nutritional Beliefs among a Low-Income Urban Population," Journal of the American Dietetic Association 42:131-135, February 1963.

142 Corsetti, George L. "Criminal Procedure-Indigents-Right to Be Informed of Right to Counsel on Appeal," Wayne Law Review 16:1446-1459, Fall 1970.

143 Cox, Donald F. "The Audience as Communicators." In Proceedings of the Winter Conference of the American Marketing Association, Boston, December 27-28, 1963, edited by S. A. Greyser. Chicago: American Marketing Association, 1964.

144 Craig, Richard B. The Bracero Program: Interest Groups and Foreign Policy. Austin: University of Texas Press, 1971.

145 Crawford, Fred R. A Comprehensive and Systematic Evaluation of the Community Action Program and Related Programs Operating in Atlanta, Georgia. Atlanta: Emory University, Center for Research in Social Change, 1969. (NTIS PB 185 939)

146 Crecink, John C., and Roosevelt Steptoe. Human Resources in the Rural Mississippi Delta with Emphasis on the Poor. Washington, D.C.: U.S. Department of Agriculture, Economic Research Service, 1970. (Agriculture Economic Report. No. 170)

147 Creson, D. L., Cameron McKinley, and Richard Evans. "Folk Medicine in the Mexican-American Subculture," Diseases of the Nervous System 30:264-266, April 1969.

148 Croneberger, Robert B., Jr. "Knowledge is Power: The Detroit Public Library." In Libraries and Neighborhood Information Centers, papers presented at the 17th Allerton Park Institute, October 24-27, 1971, edited by Carol L. Kronus and Linda Crowe. Urbana: University of Illinois, Graduate School of Library Science, 1972, pp. 125-128.

149 Cunningham, William D. "The Changing Environment and Changing Institution: Indian Project of the Northeast Kansas Library System," Library Trends 20: 376-381, October 1971.

*150 Curran, Barbara A. "Unavailability of Lawyer's Services for Low-Income Persons," Valparaiso University Law Review 4:308-325, Spring 1970.

151 Cwalina, Gustav E. "Drug Use on High School and College Campuses," Journal of School Health 38:638-646, December 1968.

152 Daniel, James. "Call for Action!--New Voice for the People," Readers Digest 95:207-212, October 1969.

153 Darity, William A. "Contraceptive Education in Family Planning." Paper presented at the annual meeting of the American Public Health Association, Miami Beach, Fla., October 25, 1967.

154 Darling, Henry R. "Inmates Say They're Not Told of Trial Date Shifts," The Evening Bulletin (Philadelphia), October 25, 1972, p. 25.

155 Darrah, Winona. "A Mobile Health Service for Migrant Families," Nursing Outlook 10:172-175, March 1962.

156 Davies, Gordon K. "Needed: A National Jobmatching Network," Harvard Business Review 47:63-72, September/October 1969.

157 Day, Grace A. "A Program for Teen-Age Unwed

Mothers, " American Journal of Public. Health 55:978-981, July 1965.

*158   Delgado, Graciela, C. L. Brumback, and Mary B. Deaver. "Eating Patterns among Migrant Families, " Public Health Reports 76:349-355, April 1961.

159   Demone, Harold W., and David F. Long. "Information Referral--The Nucleus of a Human Needs Program, " Community 44:9-11, September/October 1969.

160   Denton, Alfred M. "Some Factors in the Migration of Construction Workers. " (Unpublished Ph. D. dissertation, University of North Carolina, 1960.)

*161   Dervin, Brenda L. "Communication Behaviors as Related to Information Control Behaviors of Black Low-Income Adults. " (Unpublished Ph. D. dissertation, Michigan State University, 1971.)

162   _____. "The Research-Action-Teaching Effort at Syracuse University's School of Library Science. " In Libraries and Neighborhood Information Centers, papers presented at the 17th Allerton Park Institute, October 24-27, 1971, edited by Carol L. Kronus and Linda Crowe. Urbana: University of Illinois, Graduate School of Library Science, 1972, pp. 129-137.

*163   _____, and Bradley S. Greenberg. The Communication Environment of the Urban Poor. East Lansing: Michigan State University, Department of Communication, 1972. (CUP Report No. 15)

164   Deschin, Celia A. Teenagers and Venereal Disease. Report of a Study by the American Social Health Association, in cooperation with the New York City Department of Health. Washington, D. C.: Department of Health, Education, and Welfare, Public Health Service, Communicable Disease Center, Venereal Disease Branch, 1961.

165   Deschin, Celia S. "VD and the Adolescent Personality, " American Journal of Nursing 63:58-63, November 1963.

166   Diaz, Nelson. "¡Ahora! ¡Ahora!" [bilingual (Spanish and English) column in] The Sunday Bulletin (Philadelphia), April 15, 1973.

167   Dixon, Nellie R. "Model Cities' Own Soap Opera Offers
      Answers," Charlotte Observer, September (date il-
      legible), 1972.

168   Dobbs, Ralph C. "Self-perceived Educational Needs of
      Adults," Adult Education 16:92-100, Winter 1966.

169   Dobie, Buford, and Rene Barrera. "Why Communica-
      tion is Difficult." In Communication for Change with
      the Rural Disadvantaged--A Workshop, edited by
      Robert S. Brubaker and others. Washington, D. C. : Na-
      tional Academy of Sciences, 1972, pp. 73-77. (ERIC
      ED 060 972)

170   Dole, Richard F., Jr. "Special Problems of Consumer-
      Oriented Empirical Research in Minority Communi-
      ties," Journal of Legal Education 23:159-165, 1971.

*171 Donohew, Lewis. "Communication and Readiness for
      Change in Appalachia," Journalism Quarterly 44:679-
      687, Winter 1967.

172   _____, and Phillip Palmgreen. 'A Reappraisal of
      Dissonance and the Selective Exposure Hypothesis, "
      Journalism Quarterly 48:412-420, 437, Autumn 1971.

*173 _____, and B. Krishna Singh. "Communication and
      Life Styles in Appalachia," Journal of Communica-
      tion 19:202-216, September 1969.

*174 _____, and _____. Modernization of Life Styles,
      an Appraisal of the "War on Poverty" in a Rural
      Setting of Southeastern Kentucky. Lexington: Uni-
      versity of Kentucky, 1968.

*175 _____, and _____. "Poverty 'Types' and Their
      Sources of Information about New Practices." Paper
      presented at the International Communication Divi-
      sion, Association for Education in Journalism, Boul-
      der, Colorado, August 27-31, 1967.

176   Donohue, Joseph C. "Planning for a Community Infor-
      mation Center," Library Journal 97:3284-3288, Oc-
      tober 15, 1972.

177   _____, and Carole Peppi. The Public Information
      Center Project, Final Report, December 31, 1970.
      Baltimore: Enoch Pratt Free Library, 1971.

178 Doran, Christopher M. "Attitudes of Thirty American
     Indian Women Toward Birth Control, " Health Services
     Reports 87:658-663, August/September 1972.

*179 Dordick, H. S. Telecommunications in Urban Develop-
      ment. Santa Monica, Cal.: The Rand Corporation,
      1969. (RM-6029-RC)

180 Drennan, Henry T. "Information and Information Ser-
     vice Centers. " In Libraries and Neighborhood In-
     formation Centers, papers presented at the 17th Al-
     lerton Park Institute, October 24-27, 1971, edited by
     Carol L. Kronus and Linda Crowe. Urbana: Univer-
     sity of Illinois, Graduate School of Library Science,
     1972, pp. 91-99.

*181 Duke Law Journal Staff. "The Legal Problems of the
      Rural Poor, " Duke Law Journal 1969:495-621, June
      1969.

182 Dumpson, James R. "Family Planning and the Depart-
     ment of Welfare of the City of New York, " Bulletin
     of the New York Academy of Medicine 42:61-62,
     January 1966.

183 Dunmore, Charlotte J. "Social-Psychological Factors
     Affecting the Use of an Educational Opportunity Pro-
     gram by Families Living in a Poverty Area. " (Un-
     published Ph. D. dissertation, Brandeis University,
     1968.)

184 Eason, Helga H. "Miami, Florida, " Wilson Library
     Bulletin 44:760-763, March 1970.

185 Edgerton, J. Wilbert, and W. Kenneth Bentz. "Atti-
     tudes and Opinions of Rural People about Mental Ill-
     ness and Program Services, " American Journal of
     Public Health 59:470-477, March 1969.

186 Edgerton, Robert B. , and Marvin Karno. "Mexican-
     American Bilingualism and the Perception of Mental
     Illness, " Archives of General Psychiatry 24:286-290,
     March 1971.

187 Edmands, Elizabeth M. "A Study of Contraceptive Prac-
     tices in a Selected Group of Urban Negro Mothers in

Baltimore, " American Journal of Public Health and the Nation's Health 58:263-273, February 1968.

*188   Efionayi, Joseph A. "The Newsletter as a Communication Medium in Teaching Low-Income Homemakers, Based Upon a Study of Randomly Selected Group of Low-Income Families Participating in the Expanded Nutrition Programs in Dayton, Ohio. " (Unpublished Ph. D. dissertation, Ohio State University, 1970.)

189   Eiland, Darrell. "Citizens Information Services Dovetails Needs, Assistance, " Miami Herald, August 13, 1972.

190   Ellenbogen, Bert L. "Health Status of the Rural Aged. " In Older Rural Americans in Sociological Perspective, edited by E. Grant Youmans. Lexington: University of Kentucky Press, 1967, pp. 195-220.

191   Emmons, Karen. Welcome First-Books Later: The Service Center Branch, Richmond Public Library, December 1967-June 1971. (n. p.) 1971. (ERIC ED 060 897)

192   Employment Problems of Mexican Americans and Indians. Recommendations and Observations Made at the Southwest Employer Conference on Mexican American and Indian Employment Problems, Albuquerque, N. M. , July 10-12, 1968. Washington, D. C. : Interagency Committee on Mexican-American Affairs, 1968. (ERIC ED 028 887)

193   Endres, Mary P. "Impact of Parent Education Through Study Discussion Groups in a Poverty Area, " Journal of Marriage and the Family 30:119-122, February 1968.

194   Engel, Sophie, and Frances K. Kernohan. Community Action Program: The St. Mary's Neighborhood in the South Bronx, 1961-1966, a Report on the Five Year Demonstration. New York: Community Service Society of New York, 1967.

195   English, George E. "The Effectiveness of Emotional Appeal Versus Fact-Giving Drug Educational Films, " Journal of School Health 42:540-541, November 1972.

*196 "Eskimos of Emmonak Use Television for Record-Keep-
       ing, Cultural Assets," Journal of American Indian
       Education 11:27, 32, January 1972.

197 Ethridge, Willis A. "Needs of the Deaf: Remarks by
       Willis A. Ethridge," Hearing and Speech News 37:
       4-6, 28, September/October 1969.

198 Eyster, George W. Demonstration, Developmental and
       Research Project for Programs, Materials, Facilities
       and Educational Technology for Undereducated Adults.
       Morehead, Ky.: Morehead State University, 1970.

199 _____. Rural Adult Education. Morehead, Ky.:
       Appalachian Adult Education Center, 1972. (Issue 8)

200 Fabrega, Horacio, and Robert E. Roberts. "Social-
       Psychological Correlates of Physician Use by Eco-
       nomically Disadvantaged Negro Urban Residents,"
       Medical Care 10:215-223, May/June 1972.

201 Family Planning and the American Indian. Bladensburg,
       Md.: Westinghouse Learning Corporation, Health
       Services Division, 1971. (Focus on Health 3)

202 Farias, Hector, Jr. "Mexican American Values and
       Attitudes Toward Education," Phi Delta Kappan 52:
       602-604, June 1971.

*203 Farrington, William H. "Statewide Outreach: Desert
       Booktrails to the Indians," Wilson Library Bulletin
       43:864-871, May 1969.

*204 Feaster, J. Gerald. Impact of the Expanded Food and
       Nutrition Education Program on Low-Income Families,
       an In-Depth Analysis. Washington, D.C.: U.S.
       Department of Agriculture, Economic Research Ser-
       vice, 1972. (Agriculture Economic Report No. 220)

205 Feigenbaum, David L. "Legal Advice Publications,"
       Dickinson Law Review 76:419-443, Spring 1972.

206 Feinstein, Selwyn. "Help from City Hall: Chicago's
       Bid to Extend Services into Ghetto Wins Hopeful
       Response: Centers in Slums Offer Legal Employment
       and Assistance, 'Outreachers' Make Rounds," Wall
       Street Journal 171:1+, March 29, 1968.

207 Fejer, Dianne, and others. "Sources of Information
     about Drugs among High School Students," Public
     Opinion Quarterly 35:235-241, Summer 1971.

208 Feldman, Frances L. "Reaching Rural Alaskan Natives
     Through Human Service Aides," Welfare in Review
     9:9-14, May/June 1971.

209 Feldman, Glenn M. "Legal Rights of Prisoners," Jour-
     nal of the Missouri Bar 28:293-300+, June 1972.

*210 Feldman, Jacob. The Dissemination of Health Informa-
     tion, a Case Study in Adult Learning. Chicago: Al-
     dine Publishing Co., 1966.

211 Ferman, Louis A., and others. Negroes and Jobs, a
     Book of Readings. Ann Arbor: University of Michi-
     gan Press, 1967.

212 Ferretti, Fred. "Legal Aid Society to Train Ombuds-
     men to Serve Inmates of (New York) City's Prisons,"
     New York Times, June 1, 1971, p. 27.

213 Fetterman, Elsie, and Margery L. Kabot. "Stretching
     a Buck: Successful Public Television Series in Con-
     necticut," Journal of Home Economics 64:13-17, No-
     vember 1972.

214 Final Report of a Demonstration Project to Determine
     the Feasibility of Establishing an Information Center--
     Recreation for the Handicapped. Carbondale: South-
     ern Illinois University, 1966. (ERIC ED 022 275)

215 Finkelstein, M. Marvin. Perspectives on Prison Legal
     Services: Needs, Impact and Potential for Law
     School Involvement: Summary Report. Washington,
     D.C.: U.S. Department of Justice, Law Enforce-
     ment Assistance Administration, 1972.

*216 Fischer, Linda A. The Use of Services in the Urban
     Scene--the Individual and the Medical Care System.
     Chapel Hill: University of North Carolina, Center
     for Urban and Regional Studies, 1971.

*217 Fliegel, Frederick C., and Emory J. Brown. "Low-
     Income Farm People," Journal of Cooperative Ex-
     tension 4:44-50, Spring 1966.

218   Forman, Martin J. "The Needs of the Urban Aged in
        Two Philadelphia Neighborhoods--Factors Relative to
        Their Use of and Their Attitudes Toward Community
        Facilities." (Unpublished Ph.D. dissertation, Univer-
        sity of Pennsylvania, 1960.)

219   Forsman, Carolyn. "Crisis Information Services to
        Youth: A Lesson for Libraries?" Library Journal
        97:1127-1134, March 15, 1972.

220   Franklin, Hardy. "Reaching the Nonuser," Wilson Li-
        brary Bulletin 41:943-946, May 1967.

221   Frantz, John C. "Urban Crisis: Library Response?"
        Pennsylvania Library Association Bulletin 24:311-316,
        November 1969.

222   Freeman, H. E., and Camille Lambert, Jr. "The In-
        fluence of Community Groups on Health Matters,"
        Human Organization 24:353-357, Winter 1965.

223   "Future Opportunities for Television." In President's
        Task Force on Communications Policy, Final Report.
        Washington, D.C.: Government Printing Office, 1968.

224   Gartner, Alan. "Services: Do the Poor Use Them?"
        Social Policy 1:71-72, November-December 1970.

225   Geldard, Frank A. "Body English," Psychology Today
        2:43-47, December 1968.

226   Geller, Evelyn. "This Is My Beat: Venice Branch of
        the Los Angeles Public Library," Library Journal
        93:259-264, January 15, 1968.

227   Geller, Robert, and others, eds. "Media and Our Aging,
        Special Section," Media and Methods 9:39-49, 82,
        October 1972.

*228 Gellhorn, Walter. When Americans Complain: Govern-
        mental Grievance Procedures. Cambridge, Mass.:
        Harvard University Press, 1966.

229   Gelwicks, Louis E. "The Older Person's Relation with
        the Environment: The Influence of Transportation."
        In Transportation and Aging: Selected Issues, edited

by Edmund J. Cantilli and June L. Shmelzer. Based on Proceedings of the Interdisciplinary Workshop on Transportation and Aging, Washington, D. C., May 24-26, 1970. Washington, D. C.: Government Printing Office, 1970, pp. 19-22.

230   Gerrard, Nathan L. "Churches of the Stationary Poor in Southern Appalachia." Change in Rural Appalachia; Implications for Action Programs, edited by John D. Photiadas and Harry K. Schwarzweller. Philadelphia: University of Pennsylvania Press, 1970, pp. 99-114.

*231   Gerson, Walter M. "Mass Media Socialization Behavior: Negro-White Differences," Social Forces 45:40-50, September 1966.

232   Gillespie, Dorwin K. "Media Source Use for Health Information," The Research Quarterly 38:149-151, March 1967.

233   Ginsberg, George S., and Gary L. Starkman. "Civil Disturbances, Mass Processing and Misdemeanants: Rights, Remedies and Realities," Journal of Criminal Law and Criminology 61:39-50, March 1970.

234   Glasso, Myfanway I. Arizona Job Colleges, Inc., First Year Evaluation. La Jolla, Cal.: Systems, Science and Software, 1971. 2 vols. (NTIS PB 211 985, NTIS PB 211 986)

235   Glazer, Nathan, and Davis McEntire, eds. Studies in Housing and Minority Groups. Berkeley: University of California Press, 1960.

236   Goldfarb, Ronald L. and Linda R. Singer. "Redressing Prisoners' Grievances," George Washington Law Review 39:175-320, December 1970.

237   Goldmark, Peter C. "Communication and the Community," Scientific American 227:143-149, September 1972.

238   Goldstein, Bernard, Coralie Farlee, and Ralph Blasingame. New Bases for Library and Information Services in Metropolitan Areas: Information Usage, Beliefs, Attitudes and Exposure to the Mass Media. Washington, D. C.: U. S. Department of Health, Education, and Welfare, Library and Information Services Branch, 1972.

239 Gordon, Douglas B. "Constitutional Law--Jailhouse
     Lawyering--Judicial Sanction in Wisconsin State
     Prisons, " Wisconsin Law Review 19 2:300-311, 1972.

240 Gordon, William. "Service to Indian Reservations, "
     Minnesota Libraries 22:348-349, Winter 1969.

241 Graber, Joe B. "Community Health Services. " In The
     Daily Needs and Interests of Older People, edited by
     Adeline M. Hoffman. Springfield, Ill.: Charles C.
     Thomas, 1970, pp. 357-379.

242 Gray, Richard G. Project Public Information Finale.
     Concluding Report on a Two-Year Project Designed
     to Strengthen Information Programs in State Depart-
     ments of Education. Madison, Wis.: Department of
     Public Instruction, 1970. (ERIC ED 048 641)

*243 Grebler, Leo, Joan W. Moore, and Ralph C. Guzmann.
     The Mexican-American People: The Nation's Second
     Largest Minority. New York: Free Press, 1970.

244 Greenawalt, William S. "One-Stop Service for Poor
     Consumer, " Trial 4:38-39+, June/July 1968.

*245 Greenberg, Bradley, John Bowes, and Brenda Dervin.
     Communication and Related Behaviors of a Sample of
     Cleveland Black Adults. East Lansing: Michigan
     State University, Department of Communication, 1970.
     (CUP Report No. 13)

*246 _____, and Brenda Dervin. "Mass Communication
     among the Urban Poor, " Public Opinion Quarterly
     34:224-235, Summer 1970.

*247 _____, and _____. Use of the Mass Media by the
     Urban Poor. New York: Praeger, 1970.

248 Greenleigh Associates, Inc. An Evaluation of Total Ac-
     tion Against Poverty in the Roanoke Valley. New
     York: 1968.

*249 _____. Home Interview Study of Low Income House-
     holds in Detroit, Michigan. New York: 1965.

250 Griffin, Bobbie L., and A. Ray Blankenship. Training
     and Use of Volunteer Recruiters in Adult Basic Edu-

cation Programs. Morehead, Ky.: Appalachian
Adult Education Center, 1972. (Issue 3)

251 Griffith, C: es R., and Lester M. Libo. Mental
     Health C ultants: Agents of Community Change.
     San Fran co: Jossey-Bass, 1968.

252 Griffiths, William and Andre L. Knutson. "The Role of
     M···s Media in Public Health, " American Journal of
     Pu   Health 50:515-523, April 1960.

253 Groberg,   ·rt P. Centralized Relocation: A New
     Municipa   ·ervice. Washington, D. C.: National
     Associat: of Housing and Redevelopment Officials,
     1969. (N S PB 183 905)

*254 Gromatzsky, Irene. Consumer Education for Mexican-
     Americans. University Park: New Mexico State
     University, 1968. (ERIC ED 016 563)

255 Guthman, Judith D. Metropolitan Libraries: The Chal-
     lenge and the Promise. Chicago: American Library
     Association, 1969.

256 Haas, Mary I., and Marcile Wood. "Consumers on
     the Alert; \ Self-Help Program for Chicano Women, "
     American Vocational Journal 45:36-37, November
     1970.

*257 Haber, Lawrence D., Jack Schmulowitz, and Robert H.
     Cormier. Information and Referral Services in SSA
     District Offices: A Pilot Study. Washington, D. C.:
     U. S. Department of Health, Education, and Welfare,
     Social Security Administration, Office of Research
     and Statistics, 1971. (SS Pub. 34-71 (4-71))

258 Haggstrom, Warren C. "Poverty and Adult Education, "
     Adult Education 15:145-160, Spring 1965.

259 Hall, Julian C., Kathleen Smith, and Anna K. Bradley.
     "Delivering Mental Health Services to the Urban
     Poor, " Social Work 15:35-39, April 1970.

260 Hall, Robert E., ed. Abortion in a Changing World.
     New York: Columbia University Press, 1970. 2
     vols.

261   Halpern, Katherine S. "Navajo Health and Welfare
       Aides: A Field Study, " Social Service Review 45:
       37-52, March 1971.

*262 Halverson, Lowell K. "Report on Legal Services to the
       Indians: A Study in Desperation." In Native Ameri-
       cans Today: Sociological Perspectives, edited by
       Howard M. Bahr, Bruce A. Chadwick, and Robert
       Day. New York: Harper and Row, 1972, pp. 338-
       344.

*263 Hammond, Peter G. "Turning Off: The Abuse of Drug
       Information, " Library Journal 98:1337-1341, April
       15, 1973.

264   Hannerz, Ulf. "Gossip, Networks and Culture in a
       Black American Ghetto, " Ethnos 32:35-60, 1967.

265   Hanson, Robert C. and Ozzie G. Simmons. "Differen-
       tial Experience Paths of Rural Migrants to the City, "
       American Behavioral Scientist 13:14-35, September/
       October 1969.

266   Haro, Robert P. "How Mexican-Americans View Li-
       braries: A One Man Survey, " Wilson Library Bulle-
       tin 44:736-742, March 1970.

       Harris, Louis, and Associates, Inc. see Louis Harris
       and Associates, Inc.

267   Harrison, Gordon S. "Flow of Communication between
       Government Agencies and Eskimo Villages, " Human
       Organization 31:1-9, Spring 1972.

*268 _____. "The Mass Media in Native Villages of
       Alaska, " Journalism Quarterly 49:373-376, Summer
       1972.

*269 Harrison, Thomas J. "Training for Village Health Aides
       in the Kotzebue Area of Alaska, " Public Health Re-
       ports 80:565-572, July 1965.

270   Hart, Edward J. "Effects of Contrasting Messages on
       Cancer Control; Behavior of Females in Lower Socio-
       economic Conditions, " Journal of School Health 42:
       262-264, May 1972.

271 Harwood, Elsie, and G. F. K. Naylor. "Rates of Infor-
     mation-Transfer in Elderly Subjects, " Australian
     Journal of Psychology 21:127-136, August 1969.

272 Haveman, Robert, and others. "Midwestern Rural Pov-
     erty, Human Rights and the Need for Legal Services, "
     University of Kansas Law Review 15:513-536, May
     1967.

273 Hayes, Ann P. "Community Colleges Serve Some of
     the People, " Community College Review 1:38-43,
     April 1973.

274 _____, and George W. Eyster. "Proposal for an In-
     stitute for Training in Librarianship: Developing Pub-
     lic Library Services to Disadvantaged Adults" (un-
     published). Morehead, Ky.: Morehead State Uni-
     versity, March 1973.

274a _____, and Anne Shelby. Library/Information Ser-
     vice Needs of the Geographically Remote. Morehead,
     Ky.: Appalachian Adult Education Center, Morehead
     State University, 1973.

275 Heagerty, Margaret C., and others. "Use of the Tele-
     phone by Low Income Families, " Journal of Pediat-
     rics 73:740-744, November 1968.

*276 Health and Welfare Council of Central Maryland, Inc.
     Description of Operation of the Information and Re-
     ferral Service, 1962-1971. Baltimore: 1971.
     (ERIC ED 057 842)

277 Heath, Alice M. "Health Aides in Health Departments, "
     Public Health Reports 82:608-614, July 1967.

278 Heidt, Sarajane. "Knowledge and Its Consequences:
     The Impact of Information on a Family Planning Pro-
     gram, " American Behavioral Scientist 12:43-48,
     November/December 1968.

279 Hendrickson, Andrew, and Robert F. Barnes. "Educa-
     tional Needs of Older People, " Adult Leadership 16:
     2-4, 32, May 1967.

280 Herman, Mary W. "The Poor: Their Medical Needs
     and the Health Services Available to Them, " Annals

of the American Academy of Political and Social Sciences 399:12-21, January 1972.

281 Hiatt, Peter. "Urban Library Services for Adults of
     Low Education, " Library Quarterly 35:81-96, April
     1965.

282 The Hidden Medium: A Status Report on Educational
     Radio in the United States. New York: Herman W.
     Land Associates, 1967. (ERIC ED 025 151)

283 Hiemstra, Roger P. "Continuing Education for the
     Aged: A Survey of Needs and Interests of Older
     People, " Adult Education 22:100-109, Winter 1972.

*284 Hilaski, Harvey J. "How Poverty Area Residents Look
     for Work, " Monthly Labor Review 94:41-45, March
     1971.

285 Hill, M. Esther. "Helping Low-Income Parents through
     Homemaking Consultants, " Children 10:132-136, July/
     August 1963.

286 Hill, Robert F. "Housing the Poor: A Study of the
     Landlord-Tenant Relationship, " University of Colo-
     rado Law Review 41:541-568, December 1969.

287 Hillman, Bruce, and Evan Charney. "A Neighborhood
     Health Center: What the Patients Know and Think of
     Its Operation, " Medical Care 10:336-344, July/August
     1972.

288 Hindley, M. Patricia. "Neighbourhoods of the Air. "
     Paper presented at the International Communication
     Association, Atlanta, Georgia, April 19-22, 1972.
     (ERIC ED 061 737)

289 "Hippie Health Clinic, " Roche Medical Image 9:22-25,
     October 1967.

290 Hirschkop, Philip, and Michael A. Millemann. "Uncon-
     stitutionality of Prison Life, " Virginia Law Review
     55:795-839, June 1969.

291 Hoar, Jere R. "Reading, Listening and Viewing Be-
     havior of the Aged; An Inventory of the Mass Com-
     munications Habits and Preferences of 200 Aged

Persons in Oxford, Mississippi." (Unpublished Ph.D. dissertation, State University of Iowa, 1960.)

292 Hoff, Wilbur. The Use of Health Aides in Migrant Health Projects. Bethesda, Md.: Department of Health, Education, and Welfare, Health Services and Mental Health Administration, 1970. (ERIC ED 054 345)

293 _____. "Why Health Programs Are Not Reaching the Unresponsive in Our Communities," Public Health Reports 81:654-658, July 1966.

*294 Hoffman, Adeline M., ed. The Daily Needs and Interests of Older People. Springfield, Ill.: Charles C. Thomas, 1970.

295 Holladay, Howard P. "Communication of Mexico-Americans with Public School Personnel: A Study of Channel, Code, Receiver and Source Preferences." (Unpublished Ph.D. dissertation, University of Southern California, 1971.)

296 Holliday, Albert E. "PPI Aids Communication," Wisconsin Journal of Education 100:13-14+, January 1968.

297 Hollister, C. David. "Negro-White Differences in Parental Interest in Education," Sociological Focus 3: 96-110, Autumn 1969.

298 Holt, Marjorie P. "Help for the Disadvantaged," RQ 6:40-43, Fall 1966.

299 Honigman, John J. "Community Organization and Patterns of Change Among North Canadian and Alsakan Indians and Eskimos," Anthropologica 5:3-8, Issue no. 1, 1963.

300 Housing Monitoring Systems. Indianapolis: Department of Metropolitan Development, Division of Planning and Zoning, 1970. (NTIS PB 194 930)

301 Hoyle, Bernadette W. Information Services in Public Welfare Agencies. Washington, D.C.: Department of Health, Education, and Welfare, Welfare Administration, 1967. (Pub. No. 19)

302 Huber, George P., and Joseph C. Ullman. "Computer
     Job Matching--How and How Well," Manpower 2:2-6,
     November 1970.

303 Huiatt, A., and B. L. Hockin. "Nutrition Programs for
     Senior Citizens," Journal of Home Economics 63:683-
     684, December 1971.

304 Hulka, Barbara S. "Motivation Technics in a Cancer
     Detection Program: Utilization of Community Re-
     sources," American Journal of Public Health and the
     Nation's Health 57:229-241, February 1967.

305 "Hunger Pockets Do Exist," Austin (Texas) American,
     April 6, 1972.

306 Hungerbuhler, Gertrud. Improving Substandard Home-
     making among Low-Rent Public Housing Tenants,
     Auraria Community Center. Denver: Community
     Organization Project, 1964.

307 Hunter, Starley M. Change and Progress, A Compara-
     tive Study, Housing Project Survey, 1964-1966, St.
     Louis. Columbia: University of Missouri, Extension
     Division, 1967.

*308 _____, and others. The Families and Their Learn-
     ing Situations. Amherst: University of Massachu-
     setts, Cooperative Extension Service, 1967. (ERIC
     ED 017 820)

309 Hwang, John. "Information Seeking and Opinion Leader-
     ship among Older Americans." (Unpublished Ph.D.
     dissertation, University of Oregon, 1971.)

310 Hyman, Herbert, and Paul B. Sheatsley. "Some Rea-
     sons Why Information Campaigns Fail," Public Opin-
     ion Quarterly 11:412-423, Fall 1947.

311 Hymon, Mary W. "The Awareness and Perception of
     Adult Education as Factors in the Motivation of Adult
     on the Lower Socio-Economic Levels." (Unpublished
     Ph.D. dissertation, Indiana University, 1960.)

*312 "Information Needs of Poor Neighborhoods," Drexel Li-
     brary Quarterly 8:89-97, January 1972.

313 Irelan, Lola M. "Escape from the Slums: A Focus for
     Research," Welfare in Review 2:19-24, December
     1964.

*314 _____, and Arthur Besner. "Low Income Outlook on
     Life," Welfare in Review 3:13-19, September 1965.

315 "Is Knowledge of Most Worth in Drug Abuse Education?"
     Journal of School Health 40:453, October 1970.

316 Isaacs, Wilfred A. Community Information Services--
     1970. Cleveland: Welfare Federation of Cleveland,
     1971.

317 Jablonski, James A. "Resolving Civil Problems of Cor-
     rectional Inmates," Wisconsin Law Review 2:574-586,
     April/June 1969.

*318 Jackson, Audrey R. "A Model for Determining Informa-
     tion Diffusion in a Family Planning Program," Jour-
     nal of Marriage and the Family 34:503-513, August
     1972.

319 Jacobs, H. Lee. "Education for Aging." In The Daily
     Needs and Interests of Older People, edited by
     Adeline M. Hoffman. Springfield, Ill.: Charles C.
     Thomas, 1970, pp. 380-398.

320 Jaffe, Frederick S. "Family Planning and Poverty,"
     Journal of Marriage and the Family 26:467-470,
     November 1964.

321 Janson, Donald. "Prisoner-Aid Unit Seeks Ombudsman,"
     New York Times, May 23, 1971, p. 32.

322 Jarvis, Marilyn A., Mary Pullen, and Jane Downin.
     "Health Larnin' in Appalachia," American Journal
     of Nursing 67:2345-2347, November 1967.

323 Javelin, Muriel C. "Services to the Senior Citizen,"
     American Libraries 1:133-137, February 1970.

324 Johnson, D. L., and others. "Houston Parent-Child
     Development Center: A Parent Education Program
     for Mexican-American Families," American Journal
     of Orthopsychiatry 43:206-207, March 1973.

325 Johnson, Earl, Jr. "The O.E.O. Legal Services Program," Catholic Lawyer 14:99-111, Spring 1968.

326 Johnson, Norman, and Edward Ward. "Citizen Information Systems: Using Technology to Extend the Dialogue between Citizens and their Government," Management Science Application, Series B 19:P21-P34, December 1972.

327 Johnson, Robert W. "The Uniform Credit Code and Credit Problems of Low Income Consumers," George Washington Law Review 37:1117-1130, July 1969.

328 Johnston, Helen L., and Robert J. Lindsay. "Meeting the Health Needs of the Migrant Worker," Hospitals 39:78-82, July 16, 1965.

329 Jones, Dewey Roscoe. "Legal Services Community Education: New Profile of a Program in Evolution," Legal Aid Briefcase 29:49-57, November 1970.

*330 Jones, J. H., Jr. Evaluation of the Louisiana Nutrition Education Program. Baton Rouge: Louisiana State University, Cooperative Extension Service, 1970. (ERIC ED 041 216)

331 Jones, Mary G. "The Inner City Marketplace: The Need for Law and Order," George Washington Law Review 37:1015-1030, July 1969.

332 Jordan, Robert T., and Katherine A. Herron. "Info-U (Information Unlimited)." In Proceedings of the American Society for Information Science, vol. 8, 34th annual meeting, Denver, November 7-11, 1971, edited by Jeanne B. North. Westport, Conn.: Greenwood Press, 1971, pp. 327-329.

333 Joyce, George, and Norman A. P. Govoni, eds. The Black Consumer: Dimensions of Behavior and Strategy. New York: Random House, 1971.

334 Judd, Lewis L., and Arnold J. Mandell. "A 'Free Clinic' Patient Population and Drug Use Patterns," American Journal of Psychiatry 128:1298-1302, April 1972.

*335   Kahn, Alfred J., and others. Neighborhood Information
       Centers, a Study and Some Proposals. New York:
       Columbia University, School of Social Work, 1966.

336   Kalisch, Harriet P., and Elizabeth Baird. "This In-
       formation Service Counsels the Aged," The Modern
       Hospital 106:117-119, May 1966.

337   Kaplan, Jerome. "Voluntary Organizations." In The
       Daily Needs and Interests of Older People, edited by
       Adeline M. Hoffman. Springfield, Ill.: Charles C.
       Thomas, 1970, pp. 327-346.

338   Kariel, Patricia E. "Social Class, Age and Educational
       Group Differences in Childbirth Information," Mar-
       riage and Family Living 25:353-355, August 1963.

339   Karten, Irving. Identifying and Meeting the Health and
       Related Needs of the Aged: A Neighborhood Approach.
       Final Report. New York: Arthritis Foundation, Inc.,
       1971. (NTIS PB 207 615)

*340   Katz, E. "Communication Research and the Image of
       Society, Convergence of Two Traditions," American
       Journal of Sociology 65:435-440, March 1960.

341   Kearns, Bessie J. R. "Childrearing Practices among
       Selected Culturally Deprived Minorities," Journal of
       Genetic Psychology 116:149-155, June 1970.

342   Kegeles, S. Stephan. "A Field Experimental Attempt
       to Change Beliefs and Behavior of Women in an Ur-
       ban Ghetto," Journal of Health and Social Behavior
       10:115-124, June 1969.

343   Kennedy, Jerline, and Ruth Huey. "Homemaking Edu-
       cation for Needy Families," American Vocational
       Journal 38:20-21, April 1963.

*344   Kenney, Gerry I. People Communications in Canada's
       North. Part II: The Solution. Montreal: Arctic
       Institute of North America, 1971. (ERIC ED 060
       986)

345   Kennleyside, David. "The Fallacy of Freedom, Educa-
       tion for the Adult Eskimo," Continuous Learning 7:
       207-212, September/October 1968.

130   The Information-Poor

346 Kent, Donald P. "The Negro Aged," Gerontologist 11
     (pt. 2):48-51, Spring 1971.

*347 Kidder, Alice Handsaker. "Job Search among Negroes,"
     Labor Law Journal 19:482-488, August 1968.

348 Kline, F. Gerald. "Media Time Budgeting as a Func-
     tion of Demographics and Life Style," Journalism
     Quarterly 48:211-221, Summer 1971.

349 Knoll, Faustina Ramirez. "Casework Services for Mex-
     ican Americans," Social Casework 52:279-284, May
     1971.

350 Kochen, Manfred. "Directory Design for Networks of
     Information and Referral Centers," Library Quarter-
     ly 42:59-83, January 1972.

351 Kopecky, Frank J. "Office of Economic Opportunity
     Centers: A Critical Analysis." In Libraries and
     Neighborhood Information Centers, papers presented
     at the 17th Allerton Park Institute, October 24-27,
     1971, edited by Carol L. Kronus and Linda Crowe.
     Urbana: University of Illinois, Graduate School of
     Library Science, 1972, pp. 61-72.

*352 Kosa, John, Aaron Antonovsky, and Irving K. Zola, eds.
     Poverty and Health, a Sociological Analysis. Cam-
     bridge, Mass.: Harvard University Press, 1969.

353 Kovach, Bill. "Million in State Found to Be Aware of
     Drug Sellers," New York Times, November 23, 1969.

354 Koziara, Edward, Andrew Verzilli, and Karen Koziara.
     "Racial Differences in Migration and Job Search: A
     Case Study," Southern Economic Journal 37:97-99,
     July 1970.

355 Koziara, Karen S., and others. Labor-Force Nonparti-
     cipation of Males in Urban Areas. Philadelphia:
     Temple University, Department of Management, 1969.
     (NTIS PB 183 538)

356 Kress, Susanna. "High John Defense," Library Journal
     93:4593-4594, December 15, 1968.

357 Kuehl, Philip G. "An Examination of the Influence of

Family Life Cycle and Social Class on Information-Seeking in Self-Medication Behavior." (Unpublished Ph. D. dissertation, Ohio State University, 1970.)

358 Kurtz, Norman R. "Gatekeepers: Agents in Acculturation," Rural Sociology 33:62-70, March 1968.

359 Lachman, Sheldon J., and Benjamin D. Singer. The Detroit Riot of July 1967. Detroit: Behavior Research Institute, 1968. (NTIS PB 178 035)

360 Lacy, Dan. "The Dissemination of Print." In The Public Library and the City, edited by Ralph W. Conant. Cambridge, Mass.: MIT Press, 1965, pp. 114-128.

361 Larsen, Charles. "A Prisoner Looks at Writ-Writing," California Law Review 56:343-364, 1968.

362 Lawless, Barbara. "Press Meets Prisoners," Albuquerque Journal, March 14, 1972.

363 "Laws and Legislation Providing for the Housing of Migrant Agricultural Workers," Willamette Law Journal 6:111-130, March 1970.

364 Lee, James W., and Donald O. Covault. "Model Cities Transportation Study: Determining the Needs and Desires of Low-Income People in Atlanta, Georgia," Traffic Quarterly 26:441-459, July 1972.

365 Lee, Nancy H. The Search for an Abortionist. Chicago: University of Chicago Press, 1969.

*366 Lee, Richard L. "The Flow of Information to Disadvantaged Farmers." (Unpublished Ph. D. dissertation, University of Iowa, 1967.)

367 Lehmann, Stanley. "Personality and Compliance: A Study of Anxiety and Self-Esteem in Opinion and Behavior Change," Journal of Personality and Social Psychology 15:76-86, 1970.

*368 Leonard, J. A., and R. C. Newman. "Three Types of 'Maps' for Blind Travel," Ergonomics 13:165-179, March 1970.

369 Leonard, Olen E. "The Older Rural Spanish-Speaking
     People of the Southwest." In Older Rural Americans:
     A Sociological Perspective, edited by E. Grant You-
     mans. Lexington: University of Kentucky Press,
     1967, pp. 239-261.

370 Lerner, Steve, Wiley Hampton, and Laurel Burley.
     "Three Ballads of Reading in Gaol," Synergy issue
     no. 31:13-19, January/February 1971.

371 Lester, Eileen E., and others. "Information and Re-
     ferral Services for the Chronically Ill and Aged,"
     Public Health Reports 83:295-302, April 1968.

372 Levin, Jack, and Gerald Taube. "Bureaucracy and the
     Socially Handicapped: A Study of Lower-Status Ten-
     ants in Public Housing," Sociology and Social Research
     54:209-219, January 1970.

*373 Levine, Felice J., and Elizabeth Preston. "Community
      Resource Orientation among Low Income Groups,"
      Wisconsin Law Review 1970:80-113, issue no. 1,
      1970.

374 Levine, Ghita. "For the Elderly: Help in Finding Help,"
     (Baltimore) Sun, January 23, 1972.

375 Levy, Evelyn. "What Can I Do? Library Service to
     the Un and Underemployed," Ohio Library Association
     Bulletin 38:18-23, April 1968.

376 Levy, Sheldon G. "How Population Subgroups Differed
     in Knowledge of Six Assassinations," Journalism
     Quarterly 46:685-698, Winter 1969.

377 "Libraries Sit Down with Model City Representatives,"
     Library Journal 93:2588-2592, July 1968.

378 Lieberman, E. James. "Preventive Psychiatry and
     Family Planning," Journal of Marriage and the Fam-
     ily 26:471-477, November 1964.

379 Liebow, Elliott. Tally's Corner, a Study of Negro
     Streetcorner Men. Boston: Little, Brown, 1967.

*380 Lilienfeld, Diana M. "Mental Health Information and
      Moral Values of Lower Class Psychiatric Clinic

Patients," International Journal of Social Psychiatry
15:264-278, Fall 1969.

381 Lindquist, John H., and Charles M. Barresi. "Ghetto
     Residents and Urban Politics," Law and Society Re-
     view 5:239-250, November 1970.

382 Lindsay, John V. "Government and Community Health,"
     Bulletin of the New York Academy of Medicine 43:
     325-335, April 1967.

383 Lipsman, Claire K. The Disadvantaged and Library
     Effectiveness. Chicago: American Library Associa-
     tion, 1972.

384 "A Little PR Might Help," New York Times, April 29,
     1973.

385 London, Jack, Robert Wenkert, and Warren O. Hag-
     strom. Adult Education and Social Class. Berkeley:
     University of California, Survey Research Center,
     1963. (Cooperative Research Project No. 1017)

386 Long, Huey B. "Information Sources, Dogmatism, and
     Judgemental Modifications," Adult Education 21:37-
     45, Winter 1971.

*387 Long, Nicholas, and others. Information and Referral
     Centers: A Functional Analysis. Minneapolis:
     American Rehabilitation Center, 1971. (ERIC ED
     051 836)

388 Longman, Doris P. "Working with Pueblo Indians in
     New Mexico," American Dietetic Association Journal
     47:470-473, December 1965.

389 Lopez, Lillian. "New York: The South Bronx Project,"
     Wilson Library Bulletin 44:757-760, March 1970.

390 Louis Harris and Associates, Inc. Survival Literacy
     Study, Conducted for the National Reading Center.
     New York: 1971.

391 Lowenstein, David H., and Michael J. Waggoner.
     "Neighborhood Law Offices: The New Wave in Le-
     gal Services for the Poor," Harvard Law Review 80:
     805-850, February 1967.

392   Luce, Robert J.   "The Model Cities Community Informa-
      tion Center," American Libraries 2:206-207, February
      1971.

393   Lucier, Charles V., James W. Van Stone, and Della
      Keats.   "Medical Practices and Human Anatomical
      Knowledge among the Noatak Eskimos," Ethnology
      10:251-264, July 1971.

394   Lurie, Hugh J., and George L. Lawrence.   "Communi-
      cation Problems between Rural Mexican-American Pa-
      tients and their Physicians: Description of a Solu-
      tion," American Journal of Orthopsychiatry 42:777-
      783, October 1972.

*395 Lurie, Melvin, and Elton Rayack.   "Racial Differences
      in Migration and Job Search: A Case Study," South-
      ern Economic Journal 33:81-95, July 1966.

396   McCall, J. J.   Economics of Information and Job Search.
      Santa Monica, Cal.:   The Rand Corporation, 1968.
      (RM-5745-OEO)

397   McCombs, Maxwell E.   "Negro Use of Television and
      Newspapers for Political Information: 1952-1964,"
      Journal of Broadcasting 12:261-266, Summer 1968.

398   McElreath, Mark P.   "RFD, a New ABE Delivery Sys-
      tem," Adult Leadership 20:363-366, April 1972.

399   McElveen, Jackson V.   Characteristics of Human Re-
      sources in the Rural Southeast Coastal Plain with
      Emphasis on the Poor.   Washington, D.C.:   U.S.
      Department of Agriculture, Economic Research Ser-
      vice, 1969.   (Agriculture Economic Report No. 155)

*400 McGinn, Noel F.   "Some Correlates of Urban Knowledge,"
      Rural Sociology 36:273-295, September 1971.

401   McGraw-Hill Book Company, Inc.   Training Materials
      and Information Services Division.   Educationally
      Deficient Adults; Their Education and Training Needs.
      Washington, D.C.:   U.S. Department of Health, Edu-
      cation, and Welfare, Office of Education, 1965.

402   Macias, Ysidro R.   "The Chicago Movement," Wilson
      Library Bulletin 44:731-735, March 1970.

403 McKendry, James M. and Salvador A. Parco. The Role
     of Mass Media and Interpersonal Sources of Informa-
     tion in Directed Social Change: A Review of the Lit-
     erature on the Philippines. State College, Pa.: HRB-
     Singer, Inc., 1967. (NTIS AD 657 683)

404 Macleod, Celeste. "Prison Law Libraries and You," Li-
     brary Journal 97:3539-3545, November 1, 1972.

405 Mahan, Russ A., and Stephan R. Bollman. "Education
     or Information Giving?" Journal of Cooperative Ex-
     tension 6:100-106, Summer 1968.

406 Mahrer, Alvin R. "The Human Relations Center: Com-
     munity Mental Health from a Motivational Perspec-
     tive," Corrective Psychiatry and Journal of Social
     Therapy 18:39-45, 1972.

407 Mann, Jim. "Inmates Win Right to Quiz Parole Chief,"
     Washington Post, February 18, 1972.

408 March, Michael S. "The Neighborhood Center Concept,"
     Public Welfare 26:97-110, April 1968.

409 Marchese, Lamar. Cable Television in Central Appala-
     chia: A Feasibility Study. Morehead, Ky.: Appa-
     lachian Adult Education Center, 1972. (Issue 5)

410 Marsh, C. Paul, Robert J. Dolan, and William L. Rid-
     dick. "Anomia and Communication Behavior: The
     Relationship between Anomia and Utilization of Three
     Public Bureaucracies," Rural Sociology 32:435-445,
     December 1967.

411 Marsh, Shirley A., and Alan B. Knox. "Information
     Seeking and Adult Education," Journal of Cooperative
     Extension 4:213-222, Winter 1966.

412 Martin, Lowell A. Baltimore Reaches Out: Library
     Service to the Disadvantaged. Baltimore: Enoch
     Pratt Free Library, 1967.

413 _____. Library Response to Urban Change, a Study
     of the Chicago Public Library. Chicago: American
     Library Association, 1969.

414 Maslow, A. H. "The Need to Know and the Fear of

Knowing, " Journal of General Psychology 68:111-125, January 1963.

415 Massoth, D. "Teaching Nutrition to the Migrant Worker, " Forecast for Home Economics 17:F74+, February 1972.

416 Mayer, J. E., and N. Timms. The Client Speaks: Working Class Impressions of Casework. Chicago: Aldine-Atherton, 1970.

*417 Maynard, Eileen, and Gayla Twiss. Hechel Lena Oyate Kin Nipi Kte, that These People May Live, Conditions among Oglala Sioux of Pine Ridge Reservation. Pine Ridge, S. D.: U. S. Public Health Service, Indian Health Service, Community Mental Health Program, 1969.

418 Medved, Eva. "Television in Nutrition Education, " Journal of Home Economics 58:167-170, March 1966.

419 Mendelsohn, Harold. "What to Say to Whom in Social Amelioration Programming, " Educational Broadcasting Review 3:19-26, December 1969.

*420 _____, and others. Operation Gap-Stop, a Study of the Appalication of Communications Techniques in Reaching the Unreachable Poor. Final Report. Denver: University of Denver, 1968. 2 vols. (ERIC ED 024 788 and ED 024 816)

*421 Menzel, Herbert. "Quasi-Mass Communication: A Neglected Area, " Public Opinion Quarterly 35:406-409, Fall 1971.

422 Messaros, Henry W. "Victimized Homeowners Lose Suit; Judge Sorry, " The Evening Bulletin (Philadelphia), February 14, 1973.

423 Meyers, A. S. "Unseen and Unheard Elderly, " American Libraries 2:793-796, September 1971.

*424 Middleton, Jack, and Phil Runner. "Community Information Center, " Journal of Intergroup Relations 1:3-37, February 1972.

425 "Migrant Workers: How They Live, " TransAction 6:50-51, February 1969.

426 Miller, Charles H. "Use of Law Students in Legal Service Programs for the Poor," Tennessee Law Review 37:35-40, Fall 1969.

427 Miller, L. Keith, and L. Ocoee. "Reinforcing Self-Help Group Activities of Welfare Recipients," Journal of Applied Behavior Analysis 3:57-64, Spring 1970.

428 Miller, Robert W. "Individual Adaptation to a Changing Society: The Role of Retraining and Related Action Programs." In Change in Rural Appalachia; Implications for Action Programs, edited by John D. Photiadas and Harry K. Schwarzweller. Philadelphia: University of Pennsylvania Press, 1970, pp. 207-220.

429 Miller, S. M. "The American Lower Class: A Typological Approach," Social Research 31:1-22, Spring 1964.

430 Minear, Leon P. "Some New Approaches in Meeting the Occupational Education Needs of the American Indian," Journal of American Indian Education 9:18-22, October 1969.

431 Minuchin, Salvador. Families of the Slums: An Exploration of Their Structure and Treatment. New York: Basic Books, 1967.

432 Moberg, David O. "Religion in the Later Years." In The Daily Needs and Interests of Older People, edited by Adeline M. Hoffman. Springfield, Ill.: Charles C. Thomas, 1970, pp. 175-191.

433 Mohammed, Mary F. B. "Patients' Understanding of Written Health Information," Nursing Research 13: 100-108, Spring 1964.

434 Moles, Oliver. "Predicting Use of Public Assistance: An Empirical Study," Welfare in Review 7:13-19, November/December 1969.

435 _____, Robert F. Hess, and Daniel Fascione. "Who Knows Where to Get Public Assistance," Welfare in Review 6:8-13, September/October 1968.

436 Monroe, Margaret E. "Reader Services to the Disadvantaged in Inner Cities." In Advances in Librarian-

ship, vol. 2, edited by Melvin J. Voigt. New York: Seminar Press, 1971, pp. 253-274.

437   Montgomery, James E. "Housing of the Rural Aged." In Older Rural Americans: A Sociological Perspective, edited by E. Grant Youmans. Lexington: University of Kentucky Press, 1967, pp. 169-194.

438   Moore, John E. "Ombudsman and the Ghetto," Connecticut Law Review 1:244-262.

439   Moore, William, Jr. The Vertical Ghetto: Everyday Life in an Urban Project. New York: Random House, 1968.

440   Morrison, Denton E., and Patricia A. Phillips. A Silent Minority: A Research Feasibility Probe of Discontent among the Rural Poor. East Lansing: Michigan State University, Rural Manpower Center, 1970. (Report No. 13)

441   Munns, John G., Gilbert Geis, and Bruce Bullinton. "Ex-Addict Streetworkers in a Mexican-American Community," Crime and Delinquency 16:409-416, October 1970.

442   Mussehl, Robert C. "Neighborhood Consumer Center: Relief for the Consumer at the Grass-Roots Level," Notre Dame Lawyer 47:1093-1138, June 1972.

443   Nall, Frank C. II, and Joseph Speilberg. "Social and Cultural Factors in the Responses of Mexican-Americans to Medical Treatment," Journal of Health and Social Behavior 8:299-308, December 1967.

444   National Book Committee. Neighborhood Library Centers and Services, a Study by the National Book Committee for the Office of Economic Opportunity. 2nd ed. New York: 1967.

445   National Council of Senior Citizens, Inc., Legal Research and Service for the Elderly. Legal Problems Affecting Older Americans, a Working Paper. Prepared for the Special Committee on Aging, U.S. Senate, 91st Congress, 2nd session. Washington, D.C.: Government Printing Office, 1970.

446   National Council on the Aged, Inc. Golden Years,
      Tarnished Myth, Project FIND Report. Prepared
      for the Office of Economic Opportunity. Washington,
      D. C.: Government Printing Office, 1972.

*447 National Education Resources Institute, Inc.   A Systems
      Analysis of Southwestern Spanish Speaking Users and
      Nonusers of Library and Information Services, De-
      veloping Criteria to Design an Optimal Model Concept.
      Final Report. Washington; D. C.: 1972. (ERIC ED
      066 173)

*448 National Indian Education Association. A Design for an
      Akwesasne Mohawk Cultural Center. St. Paul: Uni-
      versity of Minnesota, Bureau of Field Studies and
      Surveys, 1972. (ERIC ED 066 192)

*449 _____. A Design for Library Services for the Rough
      Rock Community. St. Paul: University of Minnesota,
      Bureau of Field Studies and Surveys, 1972. (ERIC
      ED 066 193)

*450 _____. A Design for Library Services for the Stand-
      ing Rock Sioux Tribe. St. Paul: University of Min-
      nesota, Bureau of Field Studies and Surveys, 1972.
      (ERIC ED 066 191)

451   Naunton, Ena. "Spanish Drug Hotline Planned, " Miami
      Herald, June 20, 1972.

452   Neiman, Lois. "Legal Problems of the Aged Poor, "
      Legal Aid Briefcase 26:13-19, October 1967.

453   Nelkin, Dorothy. "Unpredictability and Life Style in a
      Migrant Labor Camp, " Social Problems 17:472-487,
      Spring 1970.

*454 Nesbitt, John A., Paul D. Brown, and James F. Mur-
      phy, eds. Recreation and Leisure Service for the
      Disadvantaged: Guidelines to Program Development
      and Related Readings. Philadelphia: Lea and Fe-
      biger, 1970.

455   New, Peter K. "An Information Service for the Aging, "
      Geriatrics 17:609-614, September 1962.

456   "New Program Offering Aid to Isolated Elderly Citizens, "
      Houston Post, January 31, 1972.

457   Newman, Emanuel H., and William H. Wilsnach.
      "Measurements of Effectiveness of Social Services,"
      Public Welfare 28:80-85, January 1970.

458   Nickerson, Gifford S., and Donald L. Hochstrasser.
      "Factors Affecting Nonparticipation in a County-Wide
      Tuberculin Testing Program in Southern Appalachia,"
      Social Science and Medicine 3:575-596, April 1970.

459   Nie, Norman H. "Future Developments in Mass Com-
      munications and Citizen Participation." In The In-
      formation Utility and Social Change. Papers pre-
      pared for a Conference Sponsored Jointly by the Uni-
      versity of Chicago, Encyclopedia Britannica and the
      American Federation of Information Processing Soci-
      eties, edited by H. Sackman and Norman Nie. Mont-
      vale, N. J.: American Federation of Information Pro-
      cessing Societies Press, 1970, pp. 217-248.

460   Niemi, John A., and Darrell V. Anderson. Television:
      A Viable Channel for Educating Adults in Culturally
      Different Poverty Groups?--A Literature Review.
      Syracuse, N. Y.: ERIC Clearinghouse on Adult Edu-
      cation, 1971. (ERIC ED 048 550)

461   Normand, William C., Juan Iglesias, and Stephen B.
      Payn. "Brief Group Therapy to Facilitate the Utiliza-
      tion of Mental Health Service by Spanish Speaking Pa-
      tients," American Journal of Orthopsychiatry 43:210-
      211, March 1973.

462   Norris, Virginia. "Educational Methods Used in Pre-
      senting Consumer Information to Homemakers Living
      in Low Income Urban Areas." (Unpublished Ph. D.
      dissertation, Ohio State University, 1967.)

463   Nyren, Karl E. "Spirit of Pikeville. The National Ad-
      visory Commission on Libraries Takes to the Road
      in Search of Grass Roots Opinions," Library Journal
      92:4465-4470, December 15, 1967.

*464 Oberschall, Anthony. "The Los Angeles Riot of August
      1965," Social Problems 15:322-341, Winter 1968.

465   O'Brien, Thomas W. "Legal Services for Prison In-
      mates," Wisconsin Law Review 1967:514-531, Spring
      1967.

466 O'Donnell, Peggy. "Books Behind Bars? a Survey,"
     Synergy, issue no. 31:8-10, January/February 1971.

467 Oettinger, Katherine B. "Public Health Aspects of Ma-
     ternal and Neonatal Narcotic Addiction," Public Health
     News: New Jersey State Department of Health 47:
     174-175, 191, August 1966.

468 Ogg, Elizabeth. Tell Me Where to Turn: The Growth
     of Information and Referral Services. New York:
     Public Affairs Committee, 1969. (Public Affairs
     Pamphlet No. 428)

469 "Ombudsmen to Aid Jailed Defendants," Long Island
     (N.Y.) Press, June 1, 1971.

470 Operation Find: An Emergency Program Conducted dur-
     ing the Detroit Civil Disturbance of Summer 1967.
     Detroit: United Community Services of Metropolitan
     Detroit, 1967.

471 Orbell, John M. "An Information-Flow Theory of Com-
     munity Influence," Journal of Politics 32:322-338,
     May 1970.

472 Oriol, William E. "Federal Role in Consumer Protec-
     tion." In The Daily Needs and Interests of Older
     People, edited by Adeline M. Hoffman. Springfield,
     Ill.: Charles C. Thomas, 1970, pp. 99-113.

473 Orlin, Malinda. "A Role for Social Workers in the Con-
     sumer Movement," Social Work 18:60-65, January
     1973.

474 Ornati, Oscar A. "Health and Poverty." In Poverty
     Amid Affluence; A Report on a Research Project
     Carried Out at the New School for Social Research.
     New York: The Twentieth Century Fund, 1966, pp.
     72-80.

*475 _____, and others. Transportation Needs of the
     Poor: A Case Study of New York City. New York:
     Praeger, 1969.

476 Osborn, Margaret O. "Nutrition of the Aged." In The
     Daily Needs and Interests of Older People, edited by
     Adeline M. Hoffman. Springfield, Ill.: Charles C.
     Thomas, 1970, pp. 235-257.

477 Ottenberg, Miriam, and Robert Buchanan. "Latest Pyra-
     mid Sales Schemes Bleed Low-Income Blacks, " Media
     & Consumer 1:10-12, March 1973.

478 Owens, Major. "The Failure of Libraries: A Call to
     Action, a Model Library for Community Action, "
     Library Journal 95:1701-1704, May 1, 1970.

*479 Padlayat, Josepi, and others. People Communications
      in Canada's North. Part I: The Problem. Montreal:
      Arctic Institute of North America, 1971. (ERIC ED
      060 985)

*480 Paisley, William J., and Matilda B. Rees. Social and
      Psychological Predictors of Information Seeking and
      Media Use, a Multivariate Re-analysis. Paper pre-
      sented at the National Seminar on Adult Education
      Research, Chicago, February 11-13, 1968. Stanford:
      Stanford University, Institute for Communication Re-
      search, 1967. (ERIC ED 107 819)

*481 Palmore, James. "The Chicago Snowball: A Study of
      the Flow and Diffusion of Family Planning Informa-
      tion. " In Sociological Contributions to Family Plan-
      ning Research, edited by Donald J. Bogue. Chicago:
      University of Chicago, Community and Family Study
      Center, 1967, pp. 272-363.

482 Palomares, Uvaldo H. "A Study of the Role of Mobility
     in the Acculturation Process of Rural Migrant and
     Non-Migrant Disadvantaged Mexican-Americans in the
     Coachella Valley. " (Unpublished Ph. D. dissertation,
     University of Southern California, 1967.)

483 Parker, Edwin B. "Information Utilities and Mass Com-
     munication. " In The Information Utility and Social
     Change. Papers prepared for a Conference Sponsored
     Jointly by the University of Chicago, Encyclopedia
     Britannica and the American Federation of Informa-
     tion Processing Societies, edited by H. Sackman and
     Norman Nie. Montvale, N. J.: American Federation
     of Information Processing Societies Press, 1970, pp.
     51-70.

484 _____, and others. Patterns of Adult Information
      Seeking. Stanford: Stanford University, Institute

for Communication Research, 1966. (ERIC ED 010 294)

485 Passett, Barry A., and Glenn M. Parker. "The Poor Bring Adult Education to the Ghetto, " Adult Leadership 16:326-328, March 1968.

486 Paul, Mary E. Evaluation of Project Late Start in Four Cities. Washington, D. C.: BLK Group, Inc., 1971. (NTIS PB 203 462)

487 Payton, Ozzie B. " A Study of Occupational Information Services Provided Vocational Students in an Inner City High School. " (Unpublished Ph. D. dissertation, University of Michigan, 1971.)

488 Penland, Patrick, ed. Floating Librarians in the Community. Pittsburgh: University of Pittsburgh, 1970.

489 Perlman, Robert, and David Jones. Neighborhood Service Centers. Washington, D. C.: Government Printing Office, 1967.

490 Peters, John M. Effect of Internal-External Control on Learning and Participation in Occupational Education. Raleigh, N. C.: North Carolina University, State University Center for Occupational Education, 1968. (Center Research Monograph No. 1) (ERIC ED 029 988)

491 Petrof, John V. "Attitudes of the Urban Poor Toward Their Neighborhood Supermarkets, " Phylon 31:290-301, Fall 1970.

492 Pfannstiel, Daniel C., and Starley M. Hunter. Extending Cooperative Extension Education to Mexican-American Families: Program, Methods and Evaluation, a Report of a Research Study, El Paso, Texas, 1962-1967. College Station, Tex.: Texas A & M University, Agricultural Experiment Station, 1968. (ERIC ED 028 005)

493 Philadelphia Anti-Poverty Action Committee. Guidelines and Program Suggestions for the Mobilization of Services to Impact Poverty in the City of Philadelphia. Philadelphia: Health and Welfare Council, 1966.

494   Philadelphia Model Cities Community Information Center.
      Internal Project Review. Philadelphia: 1971.

*495 Photiadas, John D. "The Economy and Attitudes toward
      Government in Appalachia." In Change in Rural Ap-
      palachia; Implications for Action Programs, edited by
      John D. Photiadas and Harry K. Schwarzweller.
      Philadelphia: University of Pennsylvania Press, 1970,
      pp. 115-127.

496   _____. "New Aims for Programs of Directed Change:
      The Case of Cooperative Extension in an Appalachian
      State." In Change in Rural Appalachia; Implications
      for Action Programs, edited by John D. Photiadas
      and Harry K. Schwarzweller. Philadelphia: Univer-
      sity of Pennsylvania Press, 1970, pp. 233-261.

*497 _____, and Harry K. Schwarzweller, eds. Change in
      Rural Appalachia; Implications for Action Programs.
      Philadelphia: University of Pennsylvania Press, 1970.

498   Pinkney, Alphonso, and Roger R. Woock. Poverty and
      Politics in Harlem, Report on Project Uplift 1965.
      New Haven, Conn.: College and University Press,
      1970.

499   Piven, Frances. "Participation of Residents in Neigh-
      borhood Community Action Programs," Social Work
      11:73-80, January 1966.

500   Podell, Lawrence. "Ethnicity and Education and the
      Receipt of Service," Public Welfare 30:6-11, Spring
      1972.

501   Poe, Elizabeth H. "A Spark of Hope for Prisoners,"
      Law Library Journal 66:59-62, February 1973.

*502 Pollard, M. LaRue. "Comparative Value Orientations
      and Functional Communication Behavior of Home-
      makers in Differing Socioeconomic Situations." (Un-
      published Ph.D. dissertation, University of Wiscon-
      sin, 1972.)

*503 Pomeroy, Richard, Robert Lejeune, and Lawrence Po-
      dell. Studies in the Use of Health Services by Fami-
      lies on Welfare. New York: City University of New
      York, Bernard M. Baruch College, Center for the
      Study of Urban Problems, 1969. 3 vols.

504 Ponting, J. Rick. "Rumor Control Centers: Their Emergence and Operations," American Behavioral Scientist 16:391-401, January/February 1973.

*505 Pope, Margo C. "Food Stamp Seekers Must Have Patience, Right Information," Florida Times Union (Jacksonville), April 5, 1972.

506 "Poverty Program Joins Forces with Buyer Education," Advertising Age 36:1, 87, August 16, 1965.

507 Powledge, Fred. "What We Failed to Learn," New Leader 50:5, August 14, 1967.

508 Prelesnik, John W. "An Investigation of the Inmate Liaison Role in the Informal Communications Structure in a Maximum Security Prison Psychiatric Clinic." (Unpublished Ph. D. dissertation, Michigan State University, 1972.)

509 Preloznik, Joseph F. "Legal Services for the Poor," Tennessee Law Review 37:44-52, Fall 1969.

510 Prewitt, Kenneth. "Information and Politics: Reflections on Reflections." In The Information Utility and Social Change. Papers prepared for a Conference Sponsored Jointly by the University of Chicago, Encyclopedia Britannica and the American Federation of Information Processing Societies, edited by H. Sackman and Norman Nie. Montvale, N. J.: American Federation of Information Processing Societies Press, 1970, pp. 287-299.

511 Prince, Robert J. "The Communication of Deaf Adults in a Work Setting." (Unpublished Ph. D. dissertation, University of Pittsburgh, 1967.)

512 "Prison Information Project Presses for Reform," Library Journal 97:3532, November 1, 1972.

513 "Problems of Modern Penology: Prison Life and Prisoner's Rights," Iowa Law Review 53:671-709, December 1967.

514 Program Evaluation January to July 1969; Expanded Food and Nutrition Education Program. Washington, D. C.: U. S. Department of Agriculture, Federal Extension Service, 1969. (ERIC ED 039 465)

515 A Program of Medical Service for Selective Service Re-
     jectees. Program Guidelines. (n. p.) Alameda
     County Health Department, 1966.

516 Propp, George. "An Experimental Study on the Encod-
     ing of Verbal Information for Visual Transmission to
     the Hearing Impaired Learner." (Unpublished Ph. D.
     dissertation, University of Nebraska, 1972.)

517 Putter, Harmon, and Amy Malzberg. Helping to Serve
     the Aging in Their Own Homes: The Effectiveness
     of Information and Referral Services for Meeting
     Home Health and Housing Needs of Aging Persons.
     Prepared for the Home Health and Housing Program,
     Citizens' Committee on Aging. New York: Commun-
     ity Council of Greater New York, 1969.

518 Pye, Orrea F. "Nutrition Educator in the Community, "
     Perspectives on Education 5:5-14, Fall 1971.

519 Rainwater, Lee. Behind Ghetto Walls: Black Family
     Life in a Federal Slum. Chicago: Aldine Pub. Co.,
     1970.

520 _____. "Open Letter on White Justice and the Riots, "
     TransAction 4:27, September 1967.

521 Ramsey, Glenn V., and Beulah Hodge. "Anglo-Latin
     Problems as Perceived by Public Service Personnel, "
     Social Forces 37:339-348, May 1959.

522 Ratner, Cynthia. "Educating the Low-Income Consumer:
     Some Viewpoints from an Action Program, " Journal
     of Consumer Affairs 2:107-114, Summer 1968.

523 Reaching Out to Poverty Areas: A Study of the Activi-
     ties of a Central Information and Referral Center.
     Los Angeles: Welfare Information Service, Inc.,
     1965.

524 Rees, Helen E. Deprivation and Compensatory Educa-
     tion. Boston: Houghton Mifflin, 1968.

525 Reider, Janet, Francie Bosche, and Mary H. Haas.
     "Compradores Vivarachos (Smart, Lively Shoppers), "
     Illinois Teacher for Contemporary Roles 14:109-117,
     January/February 1971.

526   Reul, Myrtle R.   "Communicating with the Migrant, "
         Child Welfare 49:137-145, March 1970.

527   Revis, Joseph S.   "Transportation and the Aging: Some
         Directions. "   In Transportation and Aging: Selected
         Issues, edited by Edmund J. Cantilli and June L.
         Shmelzer.   Based on Proceedings of the Interdisci-
         plinary Workshop on Transportation and Aging, Wash-
         ington, D. C. , May 24-26, 1970.   Washington, D. C. :
         Government Printing Office, 1970, pp. 172-180.

*528   RFD, the Six Part Series.   Madison: WHA-TV, Uni-
         versity of Wisconsin-Extension, 1972.

*529   Rich, Stuart U. , and Subhash C. Jain.   "Social Class
         and Life Cycle as Predictors of Shopping Behavior, "
         Journal of Marketing Research 5:41-49, February
         1968.

530   Richards, Jerrold R.   "Providing Legal Services to Mon-
         tana Indians," Legal Aid Brief Case 27:62-74, Decem-
         ber 1968.

*531   Rieger, Jon H. , and Robert C. Anderson.   "Information
         Source and Need Hierarchies of Adult Population in
         Five Michigan Counties, " Adult Education 18:155-175,
         Spring 1968.

532   Rieke, Luvern V. , and John M. Junker.   Evaluation of
         Legal Services for the Poor.   Final Research Re-
         port.   Seattle: University of Washington, Social
         Change Evaluation Project, 1968.   (NTIS PB 184 526)

533   Riessman, Catherine K.   "Birth Control, Culture and
         the Poor, " American Journal of Orthopsychiatry 38:
         693-699, July 1968.

534   Riessman, Frank.   "Low-Income Culture: The Strengths
         of the Poor, " Journal of Marriage and the Family 26:
         417-421, November 1964.

535   _____, and Sylvia Shribner.   "The Under-Utilization
         of Mental Health Services by Workers and Low-In-
         come Groups: Causes and Cures, " American Journal
         of Psychiatry 121:798-801, February 1965.

536   "The Right of Expression in Prison, " Southern California
         Law Review 40:407-423, 1967.

537 "Right to an Interpreter," Rutgers Law Review 25:145-
     171, Fall 1972.

538 "Right to Birth Control Information in Family Planning,"
     Social Service Review 39:96-101, March 1965.

539 Riordan, Jerome T. Study on Referrals. West Hart-
     ford: Greater Hartford Community Council, 1969.

540 Roberto, Eduardo L. "Social Marketing Strategies for
     Diffusing the Adoption of Family Planning," Social
     Science Quarterly 53:33-51, June 1972.

*541 Roberts, Don. "Tomorrow's Illiterates," Library Trends
     20:297-307, October 1971.

542 Robinault, Isabel P. Am I Hearing What You're Saying?
     --A Dissertation on the Use of the Telephone on IR
     & F. Chicago: National Easter Seal Society for
     Crippled Children and Adults, 1969.

*543 Rockwell, Richard C. A Study of the Law and the Poor
     in Cambridge, Massachusetts: Attitudes and Percep-
     tions and Use of the Legal System. Cambridge,
     Mass.: Community Legal Assistance Office, 1968.

544 Roemer, Milton I., and Daniel M. Anzel. "Health
     Needs and Services of the Rural Poor," Medical
     Care Review 25:371-390, May 1968, and 25:461-491,
     June 1968.

545 Rogers, Everett M. and Dilip K. Bhowmik. "Homophily-
     Heterophily: Relational Concepts for Communication
     Research." In Speech Communication Behavior: Per-
     spectives and Principles, edited by Larry L. Barker
     and Robert J. Kibler. Englewood Cliffs, N.J.:
     Prentice-Hall, 1971, pp. 206-225.

546 Rogers, Virginia. Guidelines for a Telephone Reassur-
     ance Service. Washington, D.C.: Government Print-
     ing Office, 1972.

547 Rogler, Lloyd H. Migrant in the City: The Life of a
     Puerto Rican Action Group. New York: Basic Books,
     1972.

*548 Roper Research Associates, Inc. Summary Report of a

Study on the Problems of Rehabilitation for the Disabled. Conducted for Warwick and Legler, Inc. on
behalf of the Advertising Council. Washington, D. C.:
Department of Health, Education, and Welfare, Social and Rehabilitation Service, 1968. (ERIC ED
042 295)

549 Rose, Arnold M. "Future Developments in Aging--Per-
     spectives." In The Daily Needs and Interests of
     Older People, edited by Adeline M. Hoffman. Spring-
     field, Ill.: Charles C. Thomas, 1970, pp. 449-463.

550 Rosenblatt, Aaron, and John E. Mayer. "Help Seeking
     for Family Problems: A Survey of Utilization and
     Satisfaction, " American Journal of Psychiatry 128:
     1136-1140, March 1972.

551 Rosenstock, Irwin M. "Why People Use Health Ser-
     vices, " Milbank Memorial Fund Quarterly 44:94-127,
     July 1966.

552 The Rural Poor and Family Planning. Bladensburg,
     Md.: Westinghouse Learning Corporation, Health
     Services Division, 1971. (Focus on Health, 1)

553 Sackman, H. "The Information Utility, Science and
     Society." In The Information Utility and Social
     Change. Papers prepared for a Conference Spon-
     sored Jointly by the University of Chicago, Encyclo-
     paedia Britannica and the American Federation of In-
     formation Processing Societies, edited by H. Sack-
     man and Norman Nie. Montvale, N. J.: American
     Federation of Information Processing Societies Press,
     1970, pp. 143-166.

*554 _____, and Norman Nie, eds. The Information
     Utility and Social Choice. Papers prepared for a
     Conference Sponsored Jointly by the University of
     Chicago, Encyclopaedia Britannica and the American
     Federation of Information Processing Societies.
     Montvale, N. J.: American Federation of Informa-
     tion Processing Societies Press, 1970.

555 Sailsbury, Lee H. "Communication for Survival--the
     COPAN Program, " Journal of English as a Second
     Language 4:25-34, Spring 1969.

556 St. Thomas More Institute for Legal Research. "Law and the Ghetto Consumer," Catholic Lawyer 14:214-225, Summer 1968.

*557 Samora, Julian, Lyle Saunders, and Richard F. Larson. "Knowledge about Specific Diseases in Four Selected Areas," Journal of Health and Social Behavior 3: 176-184, Fall 1962.

558 Sand, Michael, and Joel Weisberg. "Translating Sympathy for Deceived Consumers into Effective Programs for Protection," University of Pennsylvania Law Review 114:395-450, January 1966.

559 Sargent, Charles W. "Audio Information Transfer." In American Society for Information Science, Proceedings, vol. 7, 33rd annual meeting, Philadelphia, October 11-15, 1970. "The Information Conscious Society," edited by Jeanne B. North. Washington, D. C.: American Society for Information Science, 1970.

560 Sargent, Leslie W., and Guido H. Stempel III. "Poverty, Alienation and Mass Media Use," Journalism Quarterly 45:324-326, Summer 1968.

561 Schatzman, Leonard, and Anselm Strauss. "Social Class and Modes of Communication," American Journal of Sociology 60:329-338, January 1955.

562 Schecter, Mal. "Consumer Reviews for Nursing Homes," Media and Consumer 1:18, April 1973. (Reprinted from The New Republic)

563 Schiffman, Leon G. "Communication and Experience: The Acceptance of a New Food Product by Elderly Consumers Living in Geriatric Housing." (Unpublished Ph. D. dissertation, City University of New York, 1971.)

564 Schmidhauser, John R. "The Elderly and Politics." In The Daily Needs and Interests of Older People, edited by Adeline M. Hoffman. Springfield, Ill., Charles C. Thomas, 1970, pp. 70-82.

565 Schmutzler, Joan. Project Aurora: Preliminary Report. Elyria, Ohio: Elyria Public Library (1971?).

595   Smith, Joel, Howard P. Myers, and Herman Turk.
      "Urban Community Knowledge from a Normative Per-
      spective." In Social Aspects of Aging, edited by Ida
      Harper Simpson and John C. McKinney. Durham,
      N.C.: Duke University Press, 1966, pp. 277-285.

596   Smith, Linwood. "The Hard Core Negro Deaf Adult in
      the Watts Area of Los Angeles, California," Journal
      of Rehabilitation of the Deaf 6:11-18, July 1972.

597   Smith, Stanley H. "The Older Rural Negro." In Older
      Rural Americans: A Sociological Perspective, edited
      by E. Grant Youmans. Lexington: University of
      Kentucky Press, 1967, pp. 262-280.

598   Sneden, Lawrence E. "Factors Involved in Upward So-
      cial Mobility from the Culture of Poverty." (Unpub-
      lished Ph.D. dissertation, Michigan State University,
      1968.)

599   Social Development Corporation. Evaluation Report of
      the Emergency Food and Medical Services Program.
      Washington, D.C.: 1969. (NTIS PB 187 454)

600   Solis, Faustina. "Socioeconomic and Cultural Conditions
      of Migrant Workers," Social Casework 52:308-315,
      May 1971.

*601 Speidel, J. Joseph. "Knowledge of Contraceptive Tech-
      niques among a Hospital Population of Low Socio-
      Economic Status," Journal of Sex Research 6:284-
      306, November 1970.

602   Spitzer, Stephen P., and Norman K. Denzin. "Levels
      of Knowledge in an Emergent Crisis," Social Forces
      44:234-237, December 1965.

603   Stephens, Lowndes F. "Media Exposure and Moderniza-
      tion among the Appalachian Poor," Journalism Quar-
      terly 49:247-257, 262, Summer 1972.

*604 Stevens, David W. Supplemental Labor Market Informa-
      tion as a Means to Increase the Effectiveness of Job-
      Search Activity. Final Report. University Park:
      Pennsylvania State University, Institute for Research
      on Human Resources, 1968. (ERIC ED 024 812)

566   Schramm, Wilbur, and Serena Wade. Knowledge and the
      Public Mind: A Preliminary Study of the Distribution
      and Sources of Science, Health and Public Affairs
      Knowledge in the American Public. Stanford: Stan-
      ford University, Institute for Communication Research,
      1967. (ERIC ED 030 327)

*567 Schulman, Rosalind. "Bringing Consumer Awareness to
      the Poor," AAUW Journal 65:16-17, April 1972.

568   Schulman, Sam, and Anne M. Smith. "The Concept of
      'Health' among Spanish-Speaking Villagers of New
      Mexico and Colorado," Journal of Health and Social
      Behavior 4:226-234, Winter 1963.

569   Schwarzweller, Harry K. "Social Change and the In-
      dividual in Rural Appalachia." In Change in Rural
      Appalachia; Implications for Action Programs, edited
      by John D. Photiadas and Harry K. Schwarzweller.
      Philadelphia: University of Pennsylvania Press, 1970,
      pp. 51-68.

*570 _____, and James S. Brown. "Education as a Cul-
      tural Bridge between Appalachian Kentucky and the
      Great Society." In Change in Rural Appalachia; Im-
      plications for Action Programs, edited by John D.
      Photiadas and Harry K. Schwarzweller. Philadelphia:
      University of Pennsylvania Press, 1970, pp. 129-145.

571   Scott, Richard S., and Charles R. Allen. "Canción de
      la Raza: An ETV Soap Opera," Television Quarterly
      8:24-37, Fall 1969.

572   Scott, Robert A. "The Selection of Clients by Social
      Welfare Agencies: The Case of the Blind," Social
      Problems 14:248-257, Winter 1967.

573   Sears, David O., and Jonathan L. Freedman. "Selec-
      tive Exposure to Information: A Critical Review,"
      Public Opinion Quarterly 31:194-213, Summer 1967.

574   Seeman, Melvin. "Alienation and Knowledge-Seeking; A
      Note on Attitudes and Action," Social Problems 20:
      3-17, Summer 1972.

575   _____. "Alienation and Social Learning in a Reforma-
      tory," American Journal of Sociology 69:270-284, No-
      vember 1963.

576 Senior Advisory Service for Public Housing Tenants; Report and Recommendations to the Committee on Aging and the Committee on Housing and Urban Development. New York: Community Service Society of New York, Department of Public Affairs, 1969.

577 Seplow, Stephen. "Jailhouse Lawyer's Writs Help Prisoners to File Out (Legally)," Philadelphia Inquirer, January 11, 1972.

578 "Serving Disadvantaged Adults; An Institute for Public Librarians Held at the College of St. Catherine, St. Paul, Minnesota, June 2-13, 1969, Proceedings," Minnesota Libraries 22:275-303, Summer 1969.

579 Sharp, Lawrence J. Health-Care Seeking Behavior of Project Head Start Families, Final Research Report. Seattle: University of Washington, Social Change Evaluation Project, 1969. (NTIS PB 184 530)

580 Sharp, William. "Goals in Communication with the Disadvantaged." In Communication for Change with the Rural Disadvantaged--A Workshop, edited by Robert S. Brubaker, and others. Washington, D.C.: National Academy of Science, 1972, pp. 26-29. (ERIC ED 060 972)

*581 Sheppard, Harold L., and A. Harvey Belitsky. The Job Hunt: Job-Seeking Behavior of Unemployed Workers in a Local Economy. Baltimore: Johns Hopkins University Press, 1966.

582 Sherrill, Laurence L., ed. Library Service to the Unserved. Papers presented at a Library Conference held at the University of Wisconsin-Milwaukee, School of Library and Information Science, November 16-18, 1967. New York: Bowker, 1970. (Library and Information Science Studies No. 2)

583 Shields, Gerald R., and George Sheppard. "American Indians: Search for Fort Hall's Library Service," American Libraries 1:856-860, October 1970.

584 Shostak, Arthur B. "Birth Control and Poverty." In New Perspectives on Poverty, edited by Arthur B. Shostak and William Gomberg. Englewood Cliffs, N.J.: Prentice-Hall, 1965, pp. 50-62.

585 Siegel, Earl, and others. Determinants of Involvement of the Poor in Public Family Planning Programs. Final Report. Chapel Hill: University of North Carolina, School of Public Health, 1970. (NTIS PB 190 670)

586 Siegel, Earl, and Ronald C. Dillehay. "Some Approach to Family Planning Counseling in Local Health Departments: A Survey of Public Health Nurses and Physicians," American Journal of Public Health and the Nation's Health 56:1840-1846, November 1966.

587 Singer, Benjamin D. "Mass Media and Communication Processes in the Detroit Riot of 1967," Public Opinion Quarterly 34:236-245, Summer 1970.

588 _____, Richard W. Osborn, and James A. Geschwender. Black Rioters: a Study of Social Factors and Communication in the Detroit Riot. Lexington, Mass.: Heath Lexington, 1970.

589 Sjoberg, Gideon, Richard A. Brymer, and Buford Farris. "Bureaucracy and the Lower Class," Sociology and Social Research 50:325-337, April 1966.

590 Skrabanek, R. L. "Language Maintenance among Mexican Americans," Civil Rights Digest 4:18-24, Spring 1971.

591 "Slum Storefront Library Serves San Francisco Poor," Library Journal 95:1798, May 15, 1970.

592 Smith, Donald H. "Communicating with the Poor," Journal of Human Relations 15:169-179, Second Quarter 1967.

593 Smith, Eldon D. "Non-Farm Employment Information for Rural People," Journal of Farm Economics 38: 813-827, August 1956.

594 Smith, Eleanor T. "Public Library Service to the Economically and Culturally Deprived: A Profile of the Brooklyn Public Library." In The Library Reaches Out: Reports on Library Service and Community Relations by some Leading American Librarians, edited by Kate M. Coplan and Edwin Castagna. Dobbs Ferry, N.Y.: Oceana, 1965, pp. 213-239.

*605 Stojanovic, Elisabeth J. "The Dissemination of Informa-
       tion about Medicare to Low-Income Rural Residents,"
       Rural Sociology 37:253-260, June 1972.

606   Stough, Ada B. "The Responsibility of the Federal
       Government." In The Daily Needs and Interests of
       Older People, edited by Adeline M. Hoffman. Spring-
       field, Ill.: Charles C. Thomas, 1970, pp. 347-356.

607   Street, Paul. Community Action in Appalachia. Final
       Report 1 June-20 September 1968. Unit 12. The
       Health Education Program. Lexington: University
       of Kentucky, 1968. (NTIS PB 180 107)

608   Sturdivant, Frederick D. "Business and the Mexican-
       American Community," California Management Re-
       view 11:73-80, Spring 1969.

609   _____, ed. The Ghetto Marketplace. New York:
       Free Press, 1969.

610   Suchman, Edward A. "Medical 'Deprivation'," Ameri-
       can Journal of Orthopsychiatry 36:665-672, July 1966.

611   _____. "Social Factors in Medical Deprivation,"
       American Journal of Public Health 55:1725-1733,
       November 1965.

*612 A Survey of Health, Welfare and Recreation Services
       for Winnebago County, Illinois. Conducted by a Citi-
       zen's Committee for the Community Welfare Council
       of Winnebago County, Ill., 1968.

613   Swan, Robert C. "Indian Legal Services Programs:
       The Key to Red Power?" Arizona Law Review 12:
       594-626, Fall 1970.

614   Sweeney, Robert F. "Baltimore's Slum Housing Clinic,"
       Public Health Reports 76:693-697, August 1971.

615   Swift, David W. "Why Don't Low-Income Families Use
       Free Medical Services?" California's Health 26:6,
       October 1968.

*616 Swinehart, James W. "Voluntary Exposure to Health
       Communications," American Journal of Public Health
       58:1265-1275, July 1968.

617 Sykes, Gresham M. "The Differential Distribution of
     Community Knowledge, " Social Forces 29:376-382,
     May 1951.

618 _____. "Legal Needs of the Poor in the City of Den-
     ver, " Law and Society Review 4:225-278, November
     1969.

619 Tarrant County Community Council. Report of the
     Apprenticeship Committee. Fort Worth, Texas:
     Tarrant County Community Council, 1966.

620 Tate, Charles, ed. Cable Television in the Cities:
     Community Control, Public Access and Minority
     Ownership. Washington, D. C.: The Urban Institute,
     1971.

621 Taves, Marvin J. and Gary D. Hansen. "Programs for
     the Rural Elderly. " In Older Rural Americans: A
     Sociological Perspective, edited by E. Grant Youmans.
     Lexington: University of Kentucky Press, 1967, pp.
     281-303.

622 Taylor, Fitz J. "Adjusting the Amount and Level of In-
     formation to One's Audience, " Instructional Science
     1:211-245, July 1972.

623 Tenant's Rights, Legal Tools for Better Housing. Re-
     port on a National Conference on Legal Rights of
     Tenants. Sponsored by Department of Housing and
     Urban Development, Department of Justice, Office
     of Economic Opportunity. Washington, D. C.: Govern-
     ment Printing Office, 1967.

624 Tesser, Abraham, Sidney Rosen, Marsha Tesser. "On
     the Reluctance to Communicate Undesirable Messages
     (the MUM effect): A Field Study, " Psychological Re-
     ports 29:651-654, October 1971.

625 Thies, Barbara H. Welfare Information Service, Inc.
     Annual Report, 1966. Los Angeles: Information and
     Referral Service of Los Angeles County, Inc., 1966.

626 Thorelli, Hans B. "Concentration of Information Power
     among Consumers, " Journal of Marketing Research
     8:427-432, November 1971.

*627 Thornton, James E. "An Educational Program for Eco-
nomic-Opportunity Migrants: A Case Study in Program Development in Adult Education." (Unpublished
Ph. D. dissertation, University of Michigan, 1972.)

628 Tibbles, Lance. "Ombudsmen for American Prisons,"
North Dakota Law Review 48:383-441, Spring 1972.

*629 _____, and John H. Hollands. Buffalo Citizen's Ad-
ministrative Service: An Ombudsman Demonstration
Project. Berkeley: University of California, Institute of Governmental Studies, 1970.

630 Tichenor, P. J., G. A. Konohue, and C. N. Olien.
"Mass Media Flow and Differential Growth in Knowledge," Public Opinion Quarterly 34:159-170, Summer
1970.

631 Torrey, E. Fuller. "Mental Health Services for American Indians and Eskimos," Community Mental Health
Journal 6:455-463, December 1970.

632 Tough, Allen. The Adult's Learning Projects, a Fresh
Approach to Theory and Practice in Adult Learning.
Toronto: Ontario Institute for Studies in Education,
1971. (Research in Education Series No. 1)

633 Toyer, Aurelia. "Consumer Education and Low-Income
Families," Journal of Consumer Affairs 2:114-120,
Summer 1968.

634 Training Manual for Turnkey III Homebuyer Training.
Ogden, Utah: Thiokol Chemical Corporation, Economic Development Operations, 1970. (NTIS PB
192 492)

*635 Troldahl, Verling C., Robert Van Dam, and George B.
Robeck. "Public Affairs Information-Seeking from
Expert Institutionalized Sources," Journalism Quarter-
ly 42:403-412, Summer 1965.

636 Turner, William B. "Establishing the Rule of Law in
Prisons, a Manual for Prisoners' Rights Litigation,"
Stanford Law Review 23:473-518, February 1971.

637 Ulibarri, Horacio. Educational Needs of the Mexico-

American.   University Park: New Mexico State University, 1968.   (ERIC ED 016 538)

638 _____ . "Social and Attitudinal Characteristics of Spanish-Speaking Migrant and Ex-Migrant Workers in the Southwest," Sociology and Social Research 50: 361-370, April 1966.

639 United Community Services of Metropolitan Boston, Inc. Boston Centre for Older Americans--Third and Final Evaluative Report--October 1968 through September 1969. Boston: 1970.

640 United States. Congress. House. Committee on Government Operations. Consumer Information Responsibilities of Federal Government, Hearings before the Subcommittee on Special Studies, 90th Cong., 2d sess., 1967. Washington, D. C.: Government Printing Office, 1968.

641 _____ . _____ . _____ . _____ . Special Studies Subcommittee. Consumer Problems of the Poor, Supermarket Operations in Low-Income Areas and Federal Response, report by the Committee on Government Operations, Special Studies Subcommittee, 90th Cong., 2d sess., 1968. Washington, D. C.: Government Printing Office, 1968.

642 _____ . _____ . _____ . Education and Labor Committee. National Information and Resource Center for the Handicapped, Hearings on HR 18286 before the Select Subcommittee on Education, 91st Cong., 2d sess., 1970. Washington, D. C.: Government Printing Office, 1971.

643 _____ . _____ . Senate. Committee on Banking and Currency. Consumer Credit and the Poor, Hearings before the Subcommittee on Financial Institutions, 90th Cong., 2d sess., 1968. Washington, D. C.: Government Printing Office, 1968.

644 _____ . _____ . _____ . Special Committee on Aging. Availability and Usefulness of Federal Programs and Services to Elderly Mexican-Americans, Hearings before the Special Committee on Aging, 90th Cong., 2d sess., and 91st Cong., 1st sess., 1969-70. Washington, D. C.: Government Printing Office, 1969-70. Five parts.

*645 _____ . _____ . _____ . _____ . Consumer In-
terests of the Elderly, Hearings before the Subcommittee on Consumer Interests of the Elderly, 90th
Cong., 1st sess., 1967. Washington, D.C.: Government Printing Office, 1967. Two parts.

646 _____ . _____ . _____ . _____ . Legal Problems Affecting Older Americans, Hearings before
the Special Committee on Aging, 91st Cong., 2d sess.,
1971. Washington, D.C.: Government Printing Office, 1971.

647 _____ . _____ . _____ . _____ . Usefulness of
Model Cities Programs to the Elderly, Hearings before the Special Committee on Aging, 90th Cong.,
2d sess., and 91st Cong., 1st sess., 1968-70.
Washington, D.C.: Government Printing Office, 1968-
70. Seven parts.

648 _____ . _____ . _____ . _____ . Subcommittee
on Federal, State and Community Services. Needs
for Services Revealed by Operation Medicare Alert,
a report by the Subcommittee to the Special Committee, 89th Cong., 2d sess., 1966. Washington, D.C.:
Government Printing Office, 1966.

649 _____ . Department of Health, Education, and Welfare.
Administration on Aging. Programs on Aging--In-
formation and Referral Service. Washington, D.C.:
Government Printing Office, 1969.

650 _____ . _____ . Health Services and Mental Health
Administration. Meeting with Representatives of the
Poor, Washington, D.C., December 17-18, 1968.
Washington, D.C.: Government Printing Office,
(n.d.).

651 _____ . _____ . Indian Health Service. A Prototype Indian Health Information System: A Summary
of the Initial System Design, Tucson, Arizona. Washington, D.C.: Government Printing Office, 1969.

652 _____ . _____ . Public Health Service. Environmen-
tal Health Service. They Do a Job No One Else Can
Do: Health Educator Aide Program for Improving
Environmental Health Conditions in the Inner City.
Washington, D.C.: Government Printing Office, 1970.

653 _____ . _____ . Task Force on Organization of Social Services. Services for People. Washington,
D. C.: Government Printing Office, 1968.

*654 _____ . Department of Housing and Urban Development.
Philadelphia Housing Information Service: Report on
Experimental Project. Washington, D. C.: Govern-
ment Printing Office, 1969.

*655 _____ . National Advisory Commission on Civil Dis-
orders. Report and Supplemental Studies. Washington, D. C.: Government Printing Office, 1968.   2
vols.

656 _____ . Office of Economic Opportunity. Green Pow-
er, Consumer Action for the Poor. Washington,
D. C.: Government Printing Office, 1969.   (OEO
Guidance 6142-2)

657 _____ . _____ . Community Action Program. Community Action: The Neighborhood Center. Washington, D. C.: Government Printing Office, 1966.

658 "United States: The Chicago Fertility Control Studies, "
Studies in Family Planning, issue no. 15:1-8, October 1966.

659 Urban Information Specialist Project: An Educational
Program to Prepare Community Information Workers
in the Urban Setting: A Request for Renewal. Prepared by the Urban Information Specialist Project
Planning Committee. (n. p.)   1971.

660 Urban Market Developers, Inc. An Attitudinal and
Evaluative Study Among North Philadelphia Residents.
Philadelphia, June 1970.

661 "The Urban Reporting Project: News Media and Ghetto
Problems, " Quarterly Digest of Urban and Regional
Research 17:93-94, Spring 1970.

662 Utton, Albert E., and Francisco L. Olguin. "Indian
Rural Poor: Providing Legal Services in a Cross-
Cultural Setting, " Kansas Law Review 15:487-503,
May 1967.

*663   Verhaalen, Roman J.   "Programs of Directed Change in
       an Era of Social Reorganization: The Case of Exten-
       sion."   In Change in Rural Appalachia; Implications
       for Action Programs, edited by John D. Photiadas and
       Harry K. Schwarzweller.   Philadelphia: University
       of Pennsylvania Press, 1970, pp. 183-194.

664   Vernon, David T.   "Information Seeking in a Natural
       Stress Situation, " Journal of Applied Psychology 55:
       359-363, August 1971.

665   Vivrett, Walter K.   "Housing Needs. "   In The Daily
       Needs and Interests of Older People,   edited by Ade-
       line M. Hoffman.   Springfield, Ill. :   Charles C.
       Thomas, 1970, pp. 258-285.

666   Vogelman, Richard P.   "Prison Restrictions, Prisoner
       Rights, " Journal of Criminal Law, Criminology, and
       Police Science 59:386-396, September 1968.

*667   Voos, Henry.   Information Needs in Urban Areas: A
       Summary of Research in Methodology.   New Bruns-
       wick, N. J. :   Rutgers University Press, 1969.

668   WITF-TV.   Television and Older Americans.   Hershey,
       Pa. :   (n. d.).

669   WMCA.   Call for Action, a Guide to Problem Solving
       for New Yorkers.   New York: New York Urban
       Coalition, 1970.

670   Waddell, Jack O. , and O. Michael Watson, eds.   The
       American Indian in Urban Society.   Boston: Little,
       Brown, 1971.

671   Wade, Serena, and Adelaide Jablonsky.   Media and the
       Disadvantaged, a Review of the Literature.   Stanford,
       Cal. :   ERIC Clearinghouse on Education Media and
       Technology at the Institute for Communication Re-
       search, Stanford University, 1969.   (ERIC ED 027
       741)

672   _____, and Wilbur Schramm.   "The Mass Media as
       Sources of Public Affairs, Science and Health Knowl-
       edge, " Public Opinion Quarterly 33:197-209, Summer
       1969.

673   Wagner, Muriel G., Marqueta C. Huyck, and Margaret
      M. Hinkle. "Evaluation of the Dial-a-Dietitian Pro-
      gram," American Dietetic Association Journal 47:
      381-390, November 1965.

674   Walbeck, Nancy. "Effects of Verbal and Behavioral
      Methods of Nutrition Instruction on Changes in Atti-
      tudes, Knowledge and Action: An Experimental Field
      Investigation." (Unpublished Ph.D. dissertation,
      Northwestern University, 1972.)

675   Walsha, John P., Jr. "Attitudes and Knowledge of the
      Aged Regarding Old Age Insurance and Old Age
      Assistance." (Unpublished Ph.D. dissertation, Uni-
      versity of Southern California, 1970.)

676   Waltz, Thomas H. "The Emergence of the Neighbor-
      hood Service Center," Public Welfare 27:147-156,
      April 1969.

*677 Warner, Edward S., Ann D. Murray, and Vernon E.
      Palmour. Information Needs of Urban Residents.
      Baltimore: Regional Planning Council, April 1973.
      2 vols. (Draft)

678   Washington, Harold R. "Welfare Grievance Machinery
      in New York City," Houston Law Review 7:620-634,
      May 1970.

*679 Welbourne, James C., Jr. "The Information Potential
      in the Liberation of Black People." In What Black
      Librarians Are Saying, edited by E. J. Josey. Me-
      tuchen, N.J.: Scarecrow Press, 1972, pp. 50-59.

680   _____. The Urban Information Specialist Program:
      First Year, a Report Prepared for the Library Pro-
      fession. College Park: University of Maryland,
      School of Library and Information Services, 1971.

*681 Welfare Council of Metropolitan Chicago. Planning and
      Research Division. Human Needs in Public Housing,
      a Survey of Social Welfare and Health Services and
      Needs of Residents in Public Housing Developments
      Serving Families in Chicago. Chicago: 1970. (Pub.
      No. 4016)

682   Welfare Information Service, Inc. Project: Referral

Network--Information and Referral at the Grass Roots. Los Angeles: Information and Referral Service of Los Angeles County, Inc., 1970.

683 Weller, Jack E. Yesterday's People; Life in Contemporary Appalachia. Lexington: University of Kentucky Press in collaboration with the Council of the Southern Mountains, Inc., 1965.

684 Werner, O. James. "Law Library Service to Prisoners--The Responsibility of Nonprison Libraries," Law Library Journal 63:231-240, May 1970.

685 Wesley, Eddie. "Switchboard for Community Justice," Legal Aid Brief Case 27:155-160, April 1969.

686 Westley, Bruce H. "Communication and Social Change," American Behavioral Scientist 14:719-744, May/June 1971.

687 _____, and Werner J. Severin. "A Profile of the Daily Newspaper Non-Reader," Journalism Quarterly 41:45-50, 156, Winter 1964.

*688 Wexler, David B. "Counseling Convicts: The Lawyer's Role in Uncovering Legitimate Claims," Arizona Law Review 11:629-640, Winter 1969.

689 _____. "Jailhouse Lawyer as a Paraprofessional: Problems and Prospects," Criminal Law Bulletin 7: 139-156, March 1971.

690 Wexler, Stephen. "Practicing Law for Poor People," Yale Law Review 79:1049-1067, May 1970.

691 "What FIND Found: A Tarnished Myth," Aging, issue nos. 191-192:9, 34, September/October 1970.

692 Wheeler, Mary P. "Health Education in the Interagency Approach to Urban Renewal," American Journal of Public Health and the Nation's Health 53:63-66, January 1963.

693 White, Arthur. A Study of Neighborhood Center Programs in Rural Community Action Agencies. New York: Daniel Yankelovich, Inc., 1969. (NTIS PB 183 024)

694   White, W. James. "An Index for Determining the Rela-
      tive Importance of Information Sources," Public Opin-
      ion Quarterly 33:607-610, Winter 1969-1970.

695   White House Conference on Aging, 1971. Background
      and Issues: Facilities, Programs and Services.
      Background by Robert Morris, Consumer and Legal
      Services by Ruth Lauden, Issues by the Technical
      Committee on Facilities, Programs and Services.
      Washington, D. C.: Government Printing Office, 1971.

696   _____. Background and Issues: Housing the Elderly.
      Background by Ira S. Robbins, Issues by the Tech-
      nical Committee on Housing. Washington, D. C.:
      Government Printing Office, 1971.

697   _____. Background and Issues: Nutrition. Back-
      ground by E. Neige Todhunter, Issues by the Tech-
      nical Committee on Nutrition. Washington, D. C.:
      Government Printing Office, 1971.

698   _____. Background and Issues: Transportation.
      Background by Joseph S. Revis, Issues by the Tech-
      nical Committee on Transportation. Washington,
      D. C.: Government Printing Office, 1971.

699   _____. Section Recommendations on Facilities, Pro-
      grams and Services with Related Recommendations
      from Other Sections and Special Concerns Sessions.
      Washington, D. C.: Government Printing Office, 1972.

700   _____. The Spanish Speaking Elderly--Los Ancianos
      de Habla Hispaña. Special Concerns Session Report.
      Washington, D. C.: Government Printing Office, 1971.

701   Whitted, Harold H. "Early Detection of Cancer among
      Low-Income Groups," Archives of Environmental
      Health 6:280-285, February 1963.

702   Widiss, Alan I., and others. "Legal Assistance for the
      Rural Poor, an Iowa Study," Iowa Law Review 56:100-
      138, October 1970.

703   Wilcox, Pat. "Human Services Delivery Meets Total
      Needs of Poor, Lions Told," Chattanooga Times,
      September 7, 1972.

704 Williams, Frederick, and Howard Lindsay. "Ethnic and
     Social Class Differences in Communication Habits and
     Attitudes, " Journalism Quarterly 48:672-678, Winter
     1971.

705 Williams, J. Earl. The Role of the Community Action
     Program in the Solution of Rural Youth Manpower
     Problems. New York: New York University, Gradu-
     ate School of Social Work, 1966. (ERIC ED 020 068)

706 Williams, James D. "Communications with the Inner
     City, " Communities in Action 3:7-10, February/
     March 1968.

707 Williams, Martha. "Active and Dropout Patients of a
     Planned Parenthood Clinic System, " Welfare in Re-
     view 9:10-16, September/October 1971.

708 _____, and Jay Hall. "Knowledge of the Law in
     Texas: Socioeconomic and Ethnic Differences, " Law
     and Society Review 7:99-118, Fall 1972.

709 Williams, Martha P. "Doing It: Migrant Workers Li-
     brary. " In Revolting Librarians, edited by Celeste
     West and Elizabeth Katz. San Francisco: Bookleg-
     ger Press, 1972, pp. 63-67.

710 Wilson, Thomas D. "Advocate for the Poor: New Func-
     tion for Township Government, " Adult Leadership 19:
     76-78, September 1970.

711 _____. "Citizens Establish Ombudsman Post: Liai-
     son Officer to Serve Needs of Township Poor, " Na-
     tional Civic Review 59:334, June 1970.

712 Winick, Arthur. "New York's Automated Bloodhound:
     Computer's Job 'Scents' Lead Interviewers along the
     Placement Trail, " Manpower 2:7-9, November 1970.

*713 Wolff, Robert J. , and Bella Z. Bell. "United States:
     Knowledge, Attitudes and Practice of Contraception
     among Low Income Women in Hawaii, 1968, " Studies
     in Family Planning, issue no. 56:18-24, August 1970.

714 Wolpert, Julian. "A Regional Simulation Model of In-
     formation Diffusion, " Public Opinion Quarterly 30:
     597-608, Winter 1966.

715   Woodruff, John.   "Elderly Poor Told Use of Food Stamps
      Not First 'Handout'," (Little Rock) Arkansas Gazette,
      May 12, 1972.

716   Woods, Richard G., and Arthur M. Harkins.   An Ex-
      amination of the 1968-1969 Urban Indian Hearings
      Held by the National Council on Indian Opportunity.
      Part IV: The Indian Center.   Minneapolis: Univer-
      sity of Minnesota, 1971.   (ERIC ED 052 873)

*717   _____, and _____.   An Examination of the 1968-
      1969 Urban Indian Hearings Held by the National
      Council on Indian Opportunity.   Part V: Multiple
      Problems of Adaptation.   Minneapolis: University of
      Minnesota, Center for Urban and Regional Affairs,
      1971.   (ERIC ED 060 992)

718   The World of 207:   A Report of an In-Building Program
      Conducted in a Single Room Occupancy.   New York:
      Housing and Redevelopment Board, 1966.

719   Wynn, Barbara L.   "Oakland, California: La Biblioteca
      Latino Americana," Wilson Library Bulletin 44:751-
      756, March 1970.

720   Yahr, Harold, Richard Pomeroy, and Lawrence Podell.
      Studies in Public Welfare: Effects of Eligibility In-
      vestigation on Welfare Clients.   New York: City
      University of New York, Bernard M. Baruch College,
      Center for the Study of Urban Problems, 1968.

721   Youmans, E. Grant.   "Health Orientations of Older
      Rural and Urban Men," Geriatrics 22:139-147, Oc-
      tober 1967.

722   _____, ed.   Older Rural Americans: A Sociological
      Perspective.   Lexington: University of Kentucky
      Press, 1967.

723   Yungman, George T.   "An Experimental Comparison of
      Equivalent Pictorial-Auditory, Auditory and Written
      Modes of Disseminating Occupational Information
      among Inner City and Suburban Negro Adolescents."
      (Unpublished Ph.D. dissertation, George Washington
      University, 1969.)

724 Zahn, Jane. "Some Adult Attitudes Affecting Learning:
     Powerlessness, Conflicting Needs and Role Transi-
     tion, " Adult Education 19:91-97, Winter 1969.

*725 Zurcher, Louis A., Jr. "Characteristics of the Disad-
     vantaged as They Affect Communication. " In Com-
     munication for Change with the Rural Disadvantaged,
     a Workshop, by Robert S. Brubaker and others.
     Washington, D.C.: National Academy of Sciences,
     National Research Council, 1972, pp. 55-72. (ERIC
     ED 060 972)

Appendix A

SERIAL BIBLIOGRAPHIES EXAMINED

Abstracts for Social Workers 1967-1972

Bibliographic Index 1966-August 1972

Business Periodicals Index July 1963-March 1973

Crime and Delinquency Abstracts 1965-September 1972

Current Contents: Behavioral, Social and Educational Sciences May 17, 1972-April 18, 1973

Dissertation Abstracts through March 1973

Education Index July 1971-March 1973

ERIC System 1966-January 1973

Government Reports Announcements 1965-1972

Index to Legal Periodicals September 1961-March 1973

Information Science Abstracts 1966-1972

Library Literature 1967-February 1973

Monthly Catalog of U.S. Government Publications 1963-March 1973

Newsbank Index 1970-September 1972

Poverty and Human Resources Abstracts 1966-1972

Psychological Abstracts 1966-January 1973

Public Affairs Information Service October 1966-September 16, 1972

Selected Rand Abstracts 1963-1972

Social Sciences and Humanities Index April 1960-March 1973

Sociological Abstracts 1960-1972

Subject Guide to Books in Print 1972

Appendix B

MONOGRAPH BIBLIOGRAPHIES EXAMINED

Bates, Marcia J. User Studies: A Review for Librarians and Information Scientists. n.p., 1971. (ERIC ED 047 738)

Bolch, Eleanor, Nicholas Long, and Jan Dewey. Information and Referral Services: An Annotated Bibliography. Minneapolis: Institute for Interdisciplinary Studies of the American Rehabilitation Foundation, 1972.

Booth, Robert E.. and others. Culturally Disadvantaged; A Bibliography and Keyword-Out-Of-Context (KWOC) Index. Detroit: Wayne State University Press, 1967.

Brown, Ruth E. Community Action Programs: An Annotated Bibliography. Monticello, Ill.: Council of Planning Librarians, 1972. (No. 277)

Burg, Nan C. Rural Poverty and Rural Housing: A Bibliography. Monticello, Ill.: Council of Planning Librarians, 1971. (No. 247)

Canadian Welfare Council. Poverty; An Annotated Bibliography and References by Freda L. Paltiel. Also Supplements 1-3 by Agnes Woodward. Ottawa: 1966-68.

Copenhaver, Christina, and Joanne Boelke. Library Service to the Disadvantaged; A Bibliography. Minneapolis: ERIC Clearinghouse for Library and Information Science, 1968. (ERIC ED 026 103)

ERIC Documents Index, 1966-1969. New York: CCM Information Corp., 1970. 2 volumes.

Harding, Margaret. Helping Low-Income Homemakers: Programs and Evaluations, a Selected, Annotated Bibliography. Ithaca: New York State College of Human Ecology, a Statutory College of the State University, Cornell University, 1969.

170

Hippler, Arthur E. Eskimo Acculturation: A Selected Annotated Bibliography of Alaskan and Other Eskimo Acculturation Studies. College, Alaska: University of Alaska, Institute of Social, Economic and Government Research, 1970. (NTIS PB 197 756)

Holloway, Robert J., and Frederick D. Sturdivant, eds. Bibliography on Marketing to Low-Income Consumers.
Washington, D. C.: Department of Commerce, Business
and Defense Services Administration, 1969.

Institute for Rural America in association with Spindletop Re-
search. Rural Poverty and Minority Groups Living in
Rural Poverty: An Annotated Bibliography. Lexington,
Ky.: Spindletop Research, 1969.

Jacobs, H. Lee, W. Dean Mason and Earl Kauffman. Education for Aging; A Review of Recent Literature. Syracuse, N. Y.: ERIC Clearinghouse on Adult Education,
1970. (ERIC ED 038 552)

Jones, Dorothy M. Community Planning for Health, Education and Welfare, an Annotated Bibliography. Compiled
for the Bureau of Family Services by the Department
of Health, Education and Welfare Library. Washington,
D. C.: Government Printing Office, 1967.

Kessler, Mary Z. Ombudsmen; A Selected Bibliography.
Monticello, Ill.: Council of Planning Librarians, 1971.
(No. 186)

Lee, Donald H. A Selected Annotated Bibliography on Aging
and the Aged 1968-72. Monticello, Ill.: Council of
Planning Librarians, 1972. (No. 319)

Mangalam, J. J., with the assistance of Cornelia Morgan.
Human Migration; A Guide to Migration Literature in
English, 1955-1962. Lexington: University of Kentucky
Press, 1968.

Messner, Stephen D., ed. Minority Groups and Housing: A
Selected Bibliography, 1950-67. Storrs: University of
Connecticut, Center for Real Estate and Urban Economic
Studies, 1968.

Navarro, Eliseo. The Chicano Community: A Selected Bibliography for Use in Social Work Education. New York:
Council on Social Work Education, 1971.

Ohlinger, John. The Mass Media in Adult Education: A Review of Recent Literature. Syracuse: ERIC Clearinghouse on Adult Education, 1968. (Occasional Papers, No. 18)

Poverty and Health in the United States: A Bibliography with Abstracts. New York: Medical and Health Research Association of New York City, 1967. (NTIS PB 177 655). Also Semi-annual Supplement No. 1. 1968. (NTIS PB 196 629) and Supplement No. 2. 1968 (NTIS PB 196 630)

Poverty Studies in the Sixties; A Selected Annotated Bibliography. Compiled by the Department of Health, Education and Welfare, Social Security Administration, Office of Research and Statistics. Washington, D. C.: Government Printing Office, 1970.

Schlesinger, Benjamin. Poverty in Canada and the United States: Overview and Annotated Bibliography. Toronto: University of Toronto Press, 1966.

Stoffle, Carla J. Public Library Service to the Disadvantaged: A Comprehensive Annotated Bibliography, 1964-1968. Offprint from Library Journal, January 15, 1969 and February 1, 1969.

Straus, Murray A. and Susanne C. Graham. Marriage and Family Living, Index to Volumes 1-24, 1939-1962. Menasha, Wis.: The National Council on Family Relations, n. d.

Tompkins, Dorothy Campbell. Poverty in the United States During the Sixties, a Bibliography. Berkeley, Cal.: Institute of Governmental Studies, 1970.

_____. The Prison and the Prisoner. Berkeley: University of California, Institute of Governmental Studies, 1972. (Public Policy Bibliographies:1)

U. S. Department of Housing and Urban Development Library. Housing Markets, Selected References. Washington, D. C.: 1967.

Wasserman, Paul and others. LIST 1972, Library and Information Science Today, an International Registry of Research and Innovation. 2d ed. New York: Science Associates/International, Inc., 1972.

TOPICAL INDEX
to the Bibliography

Documents are classed by major topics under two grand categories: need and target group. The document number is listed under the appropriate topic. Document numbers are arranged in such a way that they might more easily be used coordinately, to permit the retrieval of a document by combining topics. By grouping the numbers in hundreds, it is hoped that scanning several topics for matching numbers will be facilitated. A few documents in the bibliography are not indexed below. These are documents whose relevant content is (1) very general and either (2) unsubstantial or primarily reports of demonstrations.

GENERAL

(Includes documents with the broadest coverage of information-related matters, and those that treat the life-styles and culture of the disadvantaged populations)

47	163	237	312	400	534	617	704
49	172	246	313	405	545	630	724
52	175	247	314	410	553	659	725
55	180		359	414	554	667	
85			367	421	559	671	
			376	429	560	677	
			379	431	561	686	
			386	439	566	687	
			399	468	573	694	
				471	574		
				480	589		
				483	592		
				484	598		

AREAS OF INFORMATION

Consumer Needs

19	100	213	308	442	506	608
40	116	244	331	448	522	609
41	126	254	333	449	525	620
46	133	256	357	450	529	626
47	134			462	531	633
48	143			472	532	638
91	150			473	556	640
92	161			477	558	641
	163			491	563	643
	170				567	645
	181					655
						656
						667
						677

Crisis (Includes riots and suicides)

21	136	219	350	406	504	655
	194		373	424	507	685
				451	520	686
				464	541	
				470	587	
					588	

Decision-Making (Includes problem-solving)

7	111	203	315	400	522	609	709
12	124	206	324	409	524	625	
14	128	220	326	416	529	626	
17	136	222	329	419	550	635	
34	148	228	372	421	561	638	
46	162	235		424	562	652	
47	163	253		436	563	654	
48	194	258		461	565	656	
49	196			481	567	659	
57				484	571	664	
64				489	573	667	
				493		676	
						677	
						683	

Education (Information about education)

3	103	210	308	401		632	705

Legal Matters

27	104	205	317	404	501	613	702
45	113	209	321	407	509	618	708
78	120	212	325	426	513	623	
93	127	215	329	438	530	628	
	142	217	335	448	532	636	
	150	228	361	449	537	637	
	154	233	362	450	543	646	
		236	370	452	577	655	
		239	373	465		657	
		244	384	466		662	
		262	391	469		666	
		272				677	
		286				684	
		290				685	
						688	
						689	
						690	
						695	

Political Process

20	228	326	419	510	629	710
34	243	372	438	554	635	711
88		381	459	564	655	
			470	587	672	
			495	595	686	
			498			

Recreation

217	449	620	717
294	450	644	
	454	647	
		667	
		677	

Transportation

1	229	364	475	527	667
98		368			698

Welfare Program

5	108	217	301	416	500	605	703
25	123	224	316	427	505	612	715

TARGET GROUPS

Aging

American Indian

Appalachian

81	171	230	322	409	552	603
83	173	250		410	570	607
93	174	273		458		663
96	175	274a		463		683
	198			495		
	199			496		
				497		

Eskimo (Includes native Alaskan and Aleut)

196	208	344	479	555	631
	267	345			
	268	393			
	269				
	288				
	299				

Handicapped (Deaf or blind)

1	107	203	368	511	642
60	197	214		516	
61		225		572	
62		282		596	
66					
67					
92					

Mexican-American (Chicano)

86	105	202	324	402	571	608	708
	106	243	341	415	590	638	
	108	258	349	419		643	
	147	266	369	441		644	
	169	295	394	443		671	
	186			447			
	192			482			
				492			

Migrant Workers

4	113	292	328	415	526	600	709
	119		363	425	544	627	
	132			453	552	638	
	144				578		
	155						
	158						

169	261	399	443	568	643
171	267		448	583	644
173	268		449	593	653
174	269		450	597	662
175	272		453		683
181	273		463		693
185	274a		479		
196	276		482		
198	280		497		
199	288				

Spanish-Surnamed (See also Puerto Rican and Mexican-American)

34	116	204	358	400	521	638	700
	132	254	389	420	525	696	719
	166			482	568		722
	184						